# CONTE

# ISIS AND OSIRIS
## EGYPTIAN

The fourth great Pharaoh of Egypt was called Osiris. He was a god, the great grandson of Ra who, according to the Egyptians, created the world. Tall, dark-skinned and remarkably handsome, he was one of the very best of the gods. He was even known as Onnophris which means "the Good One" for he never got drunk, he never chased women and he was a sworn enemy of violence.

Osiris took as his wife the goddess Isis who also happened to be his sister. You might think this was not a particularly good thing to do but in those days (about 4000 years before Christ) nobody would have batted an eyelid. In fact all the human Pharaohs made a point of marrying their sisters too – just to show how much they approved of the idea.

Isis was a very beautiful goddess with slender arms, a lithe, elegant body and wonderful green eyes. She would have been easily recognizable because she liked to wear a tall helmet with a gold disc set between two horns. Osiris, of course, wore a crown and carried a sceptre and whip – which were the symbols of his high office.

For many years Osiris and Isis reigned over Egypt, doing good wherever they went. The first thing they did was to stamp out cannibalism. For at that time, the people were no more than savages who didn't even know how to cultivate the land. Osiris showed them how. He also taught the men how to make bread and wine. He built the first temples and designed the first statues. He even invented two different sorts of flute.

Meanwhile, Isis was just as busy. She showed the women of Egypt how to grind corn and how to weave cloth and instructed the men in the art of medicine. She bore Osiris a son, Horus, who had the head of a falcon and was later worshipped as a sun god. It was Isis who introduced the whole idea of marriage to the people. Before that, everyone had just lived together as they pleased.

Isis and Osiris couldn't have been more popular. Nobody could have ruled Egypt more wisely. But still Osiris wasn't content.

"You know," he muttered one day, "I really think it's time I left Egypt."

"Left Egypt?" his wife cried. "Why?"

"Well, we've done a lot of good work here. But what about the rest of the world? I mean, look at Asia – just for starters. The people of Asia are still living in caves. They have the most disgusting personal habits. They never wash. They grunt at each other. I think it's time I went and did some good over in Asia."

"You're very good," Isis said. "But who will look after Egypt while you're away?"

"You will. You'll do just as good a job as me."

"If you say so."

"Good. That's settled then."

Osiris left for Asia the next day. He took no soldiers with

him and no weapons. Instead he trusted to music and kind words to win the natives over. Meanwhile, Isis ruled Egypt, keeping everything in perfect order.

But Osiris had a younger brother called Set who was his complete opposite in every way. For a start, Set was repulsively ugly with chalk-white skin, violent red hair and a pointed nose. He had pimples and he spoke in a whiney voice. Set was jealous of his older brother. He hated Osiris and wanted to be king of Egypt himself.

"The trouble with Osiris is that he's so good," he remarked one day to the Queen of Ethiopia, who happened to be a friend of his.

"What's wrong with that?" the Queen asked.

"Well, it's so boring for a start. And take this business of cannibalism. Osiris may not like it, but why should that mean we all have to stop it? Personally, I always adored a young boy lightly poached with rice. Now I'm not even allowed a nibble. And what's the harm in eating people? That's what I want to know."

"I wouldn't like to be eaten," the Queen said.

"That's not the point. I think things were much better the way they used to be. We used to have so much fun . . ."

Set would have liked to have taken advantage of his brother's absence to take over the kingdom, but Isis was so watchful that it was quite impossible. Instead he got together with seventy-two accomplices and devised a horrible plot. He pretended he admired Osiris. Whenever his brother's name was mentioned, he would smile sweetly and praise him endlessly. And when Osiris got back from Asia, he invited him to a celebratory banquet.

Because of Set's performance, Osiris suspected nothing and happily joined the seventy-two other guests at his brother's palace. It was indeed a truly delicious banquet with great heaps of food served off solid gold plates and the finest wines flowing from solid gold jugs. At the end of the meal, Set clapped his hands and four servants entered, carrying an ornate chest, lined with silver and gold and studded with jewels. Calling for silence, Set got to his feet.

"I thought I would end this feast," he said, "with a little competition. I'm sure my dear brother (whose goodness cannot be praised quite enough) will join in. The chest is both the challenge and the prize. I will give it to whomsoever can fit inside it. If you can fit inside the chest, then it's yours."

Osiris smiled when he heard this. He had noticed from the very start that all of Set's friends were rather on the fat side, although he had been far too polite to mention it. What he didn't know was that Set had chosen them for that very reason. Now he watched as one after another they tried to squeeze into the box and joined in the laughter as the task proved impossible. At last he stood up himself.

"My dear brother," he announced, "I rather fancy that I have more chance than anyone of winning your precious box. Let me try."

He walked down to the chest, got in without difficulty and lay on his back.

"There you are . . ." he began.

And at that moment all seventy-two guests leapt on the chest, slammed down the lid, locked it, wrapped it in ropes and chains and nailed it shut. Then they carried it out of the palace and, ignoring the muffled cries of protest from inside, hurled it into the Nile.

The coffin – for that was what the chest had now become – was carried out to sea by the Nile. At last it was washed up on the Phoenician coast and came to rest under a tamarisk tree. The tree reached out with its branches and embraced the chest, pulling it into its trunk. And that is where it remained for many years.

Eventually the tamarisk tree was cut down by a local king who needed a pillar to support the roof of his palace. But when the tree was set in place, it was discovered that it gave off a marvellous scent. People could smell the tamarisk tree for miles around, a smell of summer, of honey and of fresh blossoms. So remarkable was the phenomenon that news of it spread first across the country and eventually all the way to Isis in Egypt. Because of her knowledge of magic, she guessed that the tree must contain the body of Osiris and slipped away at once to retrieve it.

After the death of her husband and brother, Isis had torn her clothes and cut her hair in mourning, as custom dictated. For a long time she had searched for his body, but without success. And meanwhile, Set had seized the throne of Egypt, ruling with cruelty where Osiris had shown only kindness, enslaving the people and once again encouraging cannibal feasts. Now Isis wasted no time in cutting open the pillar and removing the chest. Once it was in her possession, she carried it back to Egypt and hid it on the floating island of Chemmis in the middle of the Nile.

There she remained, bathing the chest in tears, while she prepared the necessary funeral rites. But her misfortunes were far from over. For it happened that Set, who loved to go hunting at night, chanced to come to the island of Chemmis and to his great surprise, stumbled on the chest.

"What is this?" he exclaimed. "My dear brother seems to love me so much that he has returned to plague me. Well, this time I must get rid of him once and for all."

And so saying, he opened the casket, drew his sword and cut the body into fourteen pieces. Then he scattered the pieces across the land of Egypt and went back to the palace to sleep.

Now Isis had seen what had happened and the next two years of her life were spent searching for the fourteen pieces of Osiris. It was, you can imagine, a strange business. One day, in the middle of a clump of bulrushes, she might discover an arm and part of an elbow. Then, several months later, in a grove of palm trees, she would come across a foot or a knee. It was a complicated and gruesome jigsaw puzzle but at last the time came when she had found thirteen pieces of Osiris. The fourteenth had been eaten by a crab.

Using all her powers of magic, Isis joined the thirteen pieces together again so that the body was whole. The process that she discovered that day was called embalming and afterwards all the great pharaohs and the wealthiest noblemen were embalmed in exactly the same way which is why there have always been so many mummies in Egypt.

When Isis had finished her work, Osiris woke up as if from a deep sleep and embraced her. He could now have chosen to stay in Egypt in order to punish Set and regain the throne. But having been smothered in a chest, drowned in the Nile, swallowed up by a tree and finally cut into fourteen pieces, he was too tired and decided instead to descend to the Egyptian Underworld.

And so it was that it was left to Horus, the son of Osiris, to avenge his father's death. He and Set fought many battles, with Set becoming stronger and crueller as every day passed. But finally Horus took a sharp harpoon and plunged it into Set's brain and that was the end of him.

Horus became Pharaoh of Egypt, the last god to rule in human form. And Osiris remained with Isis in the Underworld where he ruled over the dead as kindly and as wisely as he had once ruled over the living.

# PYRAMUS AND THISBE
## BABYLONIAN

There lived in Babylon during the reign of Semiramis, two young people whose houses were divided by a single brick wall. Pyramus, who lived on one side of the wall with his parents, was seventeen years old, tall, strong and athletic. Thisbe, who lived on the other side of the wall with her parents, was three years younger, gentle and very beautiful. Not surprisingly, growing up so close to one another, the two of them fell in love. The only trouble was that the two sets of parents could not stand one another.

The reason has never been set on record and in truth it doesn't really matter, for it often happens that neighbours will dislike each other simply because they are neighbours. Perhaps the parents of Thisbe thought their neighbours surly and snobbish. Perhaps the parents of Pyramus thought their neighbours vulgar and churlish. At any rate, they never spoke. If they met in the street they would stride off in opposite directions (even if it meant going out of their way). They never mentioned one another in conversation unless it was to complain. And of course they forbade Pyramus to have anything to do with Thisbe and Thisbe to have anything to do with Pyramus.

Both Pyramus and Thisbe tried to reason with them but, parents being what they are, this proved impossible. In fact they might never have been able to talk to one another had they not discovered a crack in the wall, down at the bottom of the garden. It was not a large crack. If Thisbe squeezed her hand into it, she could just brush the fingertips of Pyramus on the other side. When Pyramus knelt down and looked through it, he could just make out Thisbe's eye gazing back at him on the other side. But at least they could talk through it and every evening they would slip away from the dinner table to swap messages in the cool night air.

But there came a time when Pyramus could bear this separation no longer. Kneeling in the moist grass with his face pressed against the cold stone wall, he sighed so loudly that Thisbe heard him on the other side.

"What is it, my love?" she exclaimed. "You sound so sad."

"This is ridiculous," Pyramus replied. "Why should we be forced to endure this simply because our parents are so stupid?"

"At least we can talk to each other," Thisbe said.

"Yes. But it isn't enough. I am seventeen years old – no longer a child. I want to hold you in my arms, close to me. I want to . . ."

"My parents would never allow it!" Thisbe interrupted. "They call you 'that awful boy from next door'. I'm not even allowed to mention your name. They have nothing pleasant to say about you."

"I know all that, but . . ." Even as Pyramus spoke, the idea came to him. "Why shouldn't we meet? Not here, but outside the city. Surely we can slip away for one night together?"

"Where?" Thisbe asked, her voice trembling.

"The tomb of Ninus. You must know it. There is a temple there, near a stream – just outside the city's boundaries."

"I know it," Thisbe whispered. "But a tomb . . . !"

"This is no time to be superstitious," Pyramus cried. "We'll meet there tomorrow night, after supper. There is a mulberry tree near the stream. You can't miss it. We'll meet beneath the tree. Oh Thisbe, my love! For just one night we will be able to hold each other and speak without fear of being overheard."

"I'll be there!" Thisbe exclaimed. "Wait for me there, Pyramus. I will come to you."

And sure enough, the following night, Thisbe wrapped a shawl around her shoulders and slipped away from her parents' house, making her way through the city to the tomb of Ninus. She went with not a little trepidation, for she would have preferred to meet anywhere other than at a tomb. It was a quiet and secluded spot, well suited to their secret affair, but somehow it seemed like a bad omen. She was going to a place of death. Would death be awaiting her when she got there?

She crossed an ancient copse on the outskirts of the city, her feet making no sound on the thick carpet of moss. The moon was full that night, its ivory beams breaking through the branches and casting a thousand leafy shadows on the ground below. Now she could hear the gurgle of a stream and hurrying forward she saw two marble columns rising smooth and graceful out of the grass on the edge of a clearing. It was the tomb of Ninus, and there was the mulberry tree, its fruit as white as snow in the moonlight. But there was no sign of Pyramus. She stopped in front of the entrance to the tomb, a great iron ring hanging just above her head on the wooden door. Still nobody came. A cloud shaped like a pointed finger slid in front of the moon. A gust of wind tussled her hair.

Then she heard the sound, a soft, menacing growl. It came from the wood. Stepping back, she crouched in the shadow of the tomb as a great animal padded silently out from amongst the trees. It was a lioness and it had recently killed, for the blood was still fresh on its muzzle.

"Oh Pyramus, Pyramus!" Thisbe moaned to herself. She could hardly move, paralysed with fear.

The lioness heard her. Its head twisted towards her. Thisbe's hand reached out and tugged at the iron ring set in the door of the tomb. The door creaked open. Then, her eyes never leaving the lioness, she stepped backwards into the blackness of the tomb, slamming the door shut a moment later.

The animal had no intention of harming Thisbe, although she was not to know that. It had eaten already but, hearing the noise, it stalked across the clearing to investigate. Thisbe was out of its sight but as she had reached for the iron ring her shawl had slipped off her shoulders and this the lioness found. As much out of curiosity as anger, it raked at the shawl with its claws, tearing it. A few drops of blood dripped off its mouth, staining it. Then, forgetting all about Thisbe, it re-crossed the clearing and went to the stream to drink.

Meanwhile, Pyramus had been delayed at the supper table by his parents. Although he had asked to be excused several times, they had both had a bad day and were taking it out on him, complaining about his appearance, his lack of ambition, his poor results at school – just about anything they could think of. At last they dismissed him and he was able to steal from the house, make his way through the city and race out to the tomb of Ninus. He didn't stop running until he saw the mulberry tree. At the same moment, he saw the lioness.

The animal, having eaten and drunk, was fast asleep. Lying in the moonlight, you could almost have mistaken it for a statue but for the rise and fall of its stomach and the gleam of blood around its mouth. Pyramus saw the blood. A second later he saw Thisbe's shawl, torn and blood-stained on the grass. He looked back at the lioness. Obviously it had recently feasted. There was no sign of Thisbe. Pyramus raised his head to the sky and wailed.

His parents had denied him love's joy. Now they were unable to spare him love's pain. He felt as if an ice-cold dagger had been plunged into his heart. The life drained out of him – or if not the life then the need to live. It was as if he were suddenly seeing the world in black and white and knew that he would never again understand or experience colour. He had loved Thisbe as much as any man can love any woman and her death made no sense of his life.

Worse still, he was to blame. If he had arrived sooner, if he had got there first, then armed with his sword he would have been able to . . .

His sword. He took it from his waist and holding it in both hands, thrust it into his side. He fell back on the grass beneath the mulberry tree. There was no pain but his blood burst out in a fountain, spraying the mulberry fruit. At the same time, a pool of blood formed around him, sinking into the earth and soaking the roots of the tree.

It was then that Thisbe came out of the tomb. She had waited there as long as she could but at last the inky blackness and the damp smell of the grave had driven her out. Slowly she stepped back into the moonlight, searching for the lioness. She frowned. The mulberry tree was still there, but now its fruit was not white but red. What had happened? Pyramus groaned. Thisbe cried out and, forgetting the lioness, ran to him.

Pyramus was dying, but still he was not quite dead. As Thisbe threw herself down beside him, tears streaming down her cheeks, his eyes widened in surprise and he tried to speak. But the words faded on his lips.

"Pyramus!" Thisbe wept. "What has happened? Tell me! How can this have happened?"

With a trembling hand, Pyramus pointed to the torn shawl. He raised the hand and stroked her cheek. Even now he smiled, feeling her soft flesh without the wall between them. Then his eyes closed and he died.

Thisbe understood what had happened.

"You killed yourself!" she whispered, the tears falling faster. "You thought me dead and died rather than live without me. But death will not separate us."

She reached out and grasped the sword, turning it towards her breast. Then she looked up for a last time. Overhead, the stars were sparkling in the night sky.

"I ask the gods only this!" she cried. "The mulberry tree is stained with my love's blood. May it stay that colour to remind the world of what has happened here."

She threw herself forward onto the sword.

When their parents discovered the two bodies, they had them cremated and then collected the ashes and mixed them together in a single urn. The gods, too, were moved to pity, for to this day the fruit of the mulberry tree is not white but dark purple, and so it will always be.

# THE JUDGEMENT OF PARIS
## GREEK

The intrigues of the gods of Ancient Greece often had far-reaching effects on the affairs of men. So unpredictable were the divine inhabitants of Mount Olympus that what might begin the day as a happy occasion, a cause for celebration, might by sunset have been transformed into a bloodbath that would cast crimson shadows over the world for years to come. Just such an event was the marriage of Peleus and Thetis. For it was a signpost on the road that would lead, through so many twists and turns, to the nine terrible years of the Trojan War.

*Peleus and Thetis*

Thetis was one of the most beautiful of the Nereids, the immortal nymphs of the sea. So beautiful was she that Zeus, the king of the gods, had fallen in love with her. But she had coldly rejected him, partly because Zeus was rather fat with a huge, bushy beard, but also because he was married to Hera who happened to be her foster mother. To get his revenge, Zeus had decreed that Thetis would never marry an immortal. Hera had then chosen Peleus for her.

Peleus was a king: young, handsome and the owner of a magic sword that made him the victor of any battle he fought.

"He may not be immortal," Hera said. "But, my dear,

he's about as close as you're going to get."

Thetis, furious at the thought of having to marry a mere human being, took herself off to a secluded island, riding naked across the sea on the back of a dolphin. But when she got there she found Peleus waiting for her. At once he threw himself on her, kissing her passionately. Thetis turned herself into fire. Peleus hung on. She turned herself into water. Peleus wouldn't let go. She became a lion, a serpent – even an octopus. Still Peleus clung to her even though he was by now burnt, drenched, clawed, bitten, covered in ink and very tired. At last Thetis yielded to him and discovered that Hera had indeed been telling the truth.

Never was there a wedding like that of Peleus and Thetis. It was celebrated at midnight on the gentle slopes of Mount Pelion. As the couple exchanged their vows, they were lit by a full moon, by a confetti of stars and by a ring of blazing lamps, swaying in the olive trees. After the heat of the day, the breeze was soft and cool. Gods walked side by side with mortals, breathing in the scented midnight air. Centaurs cantered in the long grass with laughing Nereids on their backs. The nine Muses came down from heaven to sing the nuptials. The beautiful Ganymedes himself, cup-bearer to the gods, poured nectar from a silver jug. For a short time the world was still and Peleus and Thetis were in love.

There was one goddess who had not been invited to the wedding. Her name was Eris and as she was the goddess of strife and discord, nobody had wanted her to come. Now she appeared, her long, grey hair sprawling over her shrivelled face, her eyes aflame. In one skeletal hand she held a golden apple. As the music died down and the guests stared at her, she lifted it up. For a moment the moonlight caught the gold and it seemed to explode, white, above her head. Then, with a shrill laugh, she threw it down onto the ground and without a word turned back the way she had come.

The apple hit the ground and rolled down a slope to rest at the feet of three goddesses who had been talking together, arm in arm, when Eris had arrived. The three were Athene, goddess of wisdom, Aphrodite, goddess of love, and Hera. It was Hera who broke the silence.

"A present from Eris!" she exclaimed, "Why don't you pick it up, Peleus?"

Peleus leant down. As his palm surrounded it, the chill of the metal seemed to travel up his arm, shuddering through his veins until it reached his very heart.

It was far heavier than he would have thought possible. In seconds his wrists and shoulders were aching. He would have gladly thrown it away from him. Although the apple was made of gold it was somehow ugly. He could almost feel it draining the life out of him.

"Is there an inscription?" Athene asked. "Who is it for?"

Peleus turned the apple clumsily in his hands. "Yes," he said. He could not lie. "There is an inscription."

"What does it say?" Aphrodite demanded.

"It . . . it . . . " The words died in his throat. Despite the breeze, he was sweating. He looked again at the three simple words cut into the gold surface of the apple. Three words. "To the fairest," he read out.

"To the fairest," Hera repeated.

"The fairest," Aphrodite muttered, smiling.

"And to which one of us are you going to give it?" Athene asked.

"I . . . I don't know."

There often comes a moment at a party when something goes wrong and you know that no matter what you say or how much more wine you drink, nothing is going to make it right. That moment had now come to the wedding of Peleus and Thetis. Although the three goddesses were still smiling, their arms were no longer linked and their eyes were firmly fixed on the apple. The guests had formed a wide circle around them. Nobody was talking. Then Zeus stepped forward.

"We will not decide who deserves the apple tonight," he said. "That decision can be made at another time."

"By whom?" Athene demanded.

"If you decide, you'll just give it to your wife," Aphrodite said.

"And why not?" Hera cried. "It was probably meant for me anyway."

"A man shall decide," Zeus interrupted. "Paris, son of Priam, will be the judge."

He took the apple from Peleus. Peleus stepped back, rubbing his palm. He looked up and shivered. A cloud had passed across the face of the moon. Suddenly it was cold.

### Paris

Paris was the son of Priam and Hecuba, the king and queen of Troy. A few weeks before he had been born, his mother had had a horrible nightmare. She had dreamt that instead of a baby, she had given birth to a blazing log. The log had fallen to the ground in a shower of sparks and from the crumbling wood had emerged a flood of fiery worms. She had awoken screaming that Troy was on fire and it was days before she was able to sleep again. Priam had consulted a seer to find out what the dream meant and this was what he was told:

"The child that is about to be born will destroy our country. If you do not want to see Troy in ruins and the blood of your other children coagulating in the mud then, mighty Priam, you must kill him immediately!"

When he heard the prophecy, Priam determined to kill the child himself. But when, a few days later, his wife delivered a healthy, gurgling boy, he could not find the heart to do it. Instead he gave the task to a man called Agelaus, who was his chief shepherd. Although Agelaus wasn't particularly happy about the order, he dared not disobey and left the child on a barren slope on Mount Ida, thinking he would quickly starve to death. But returning there five days later, he was astonished to find him still alive, for the boy had been suckled by a she-bear. With a sigh, he drew his sword. The baby laughed at him and his heart melted. Carrying the boy home in a wallet, he sent a dog's tongue to Priam, telling him that it came from his dead baby. He brought the boy up as his own son, calling him Paris which is the Greek word for wallet.

Nobody ever really believed that Paris was the true son of Agelaus. He was far too strong and quick-witted to be the son of a mere shepherd. But it was as a shepherd that he had been brought up. And it was while he was guarding his adoptive father's sheep on the heights of Mount Gargarus that Hermes, the messenger of the gods, came to him, accompanied by Hera, Athene and Aphrodite.

"Paris!" the messenger god exclaimed as his winged sandals carried him gently through the air. "I come from Zeus, lord of Olympus. He has chosen you from all the mortals in the world to make a judgement." He reached into his satchel and produced the apple. "You must give this to one of the three goddesses that you see before you. But it is up to you to decide which is the fairest. For it is to the fairest of the three that this prize must be awarded."

Paris took the apple, gazing at the three goddesses who were by this time neither holding hands, smiling nor even looking at one another.

"How can I honestly choose between three such lovely creatures?" he asked. "Why can't I cut the apple in three?" He looked at the gleaming gold. "That way I could give them each a third and even keep a couple of pips for myself."

"You must do as Zeus instructs," Hermes said. "Think carefully and choose."

"Very well," Paris sighed. And thought.

*Hera*

As well as being the wife of Zeus, Hera was also his sister. She sat on a golden throne beside him on Mount Olympus, doing her best to ignore his many love affairs. But she was never unfaithful to him herself.

She had appeared to Paris as a young woman wearing a long, simple tunic with a crown of leaves and blossoms on her head and two magnificent earrings, each one made of three brilliant diamonds, hanging from her ears. Hera took great care of her looks. Being married to Zeus who ran after just about every nymph, nereid and goddess that he saw (not to mention a fair number of young men too), she had no choice. Once a year she took herself off to swim in the magical waters of the spring of Canathus and when she returned, even Zeus would have to admit that she was lovelier than ever.

She was known as the goddess of the white arms, and as she walked in front of the young shepherd, he could not help but wonder at the purity of her skin. A peacock, her sacred animal, walked beside her, its tail open to exhibit an explosion of turquoise and emerald as if it thought that it could lend some of its own beauty to that of its mistress.

"Paris," she said, stopping and throwing back her hair. "I think you should think very, very carefully before you make up your mind. Far be it from me to influence your decision, but you might like to consider just how unwise it might be to have the wife of Zeus as your enemy. Poor Semele, for example . . . I had her burnt to death. I turned Io into a cow, which I suppose was appropriate. As for Hercules, well he'd gone right out of his mind by the time I'd finished with him.

"On the other hand," and here she smiled sweetly, "my generosity knows no bounds. How would you like to be the lord of all Asia, just for a start? Here you are working as a humble shepherd. I could make you the richest man in the world. Choose me, Paris. I am the fairest. The apple is rightfully mine."

### Athene

Athene was taller and thinner than Hera and wore neither jewellery nor ornament, carrying instead a sword and a shield. Until she had undressed, she had been wearing a rough cloak over a suit of armour with her head encased in a silver helmet. A face of unbelievable hideousness stared out of her shield which she now laid in the grass so as not to upset Paris. This was Medusa who had at one time been able to turn people into stone until, with Athene's help, she had been decapitated.

The goddess of wisdom (and, on occasion, of war) was the daughter of Zeus and Metis, his first wife. She had been born in a very peculiar way. For Zeus, after an argument, had swallowed Metis whole. Everybody on Mount Olympus had been far too polite to mention this, and when Zeus went to bed with a blinding headache, they had all assumed it was guilt. In fact it was Athene who leapt out of her father's head to his great astonishment but also, it must be said, to his relief.

Unlike virtually all the other gods and goddesses, Athene was completely chaste. When a young man, Tiresias, had accidentally spotted her swimming in the nude, she had immediately struck him blind. You can imagine, then, that she was hardly happy about parading herself in front of Paris and when she spoke she was short and sharp.

"Choose with wisdom, young man," she said. "So choose the goddess of wisdom. Choose me! . . . Gifts? What would the wife of Zeus know about gifts? Nothing! Who was it who gave mankind the first chariots, tamed the first horses, invented the pottery wheel and taught the art of weaving? Not old ivory-arms, I can tell you! Choose me and I will give you great wisdom. Choose me and you will never lose a battle."

"I'm not sure I ever want to fight a battle," Paris said. "But thank you all the same."

### Aphrodite

The third goddess was no more beautiful than the other two but somehow Paris found himself most swiftly drawn to her. For Aphrodite was the goddess of love. The owner of a magic girdle that could instantly enslave god or man, she was the complete mistress of the art of seduction, a laughing, shameless, secretive immortal both envied and admired by her sisters on Mount Olympus.

And yet she was married to one of the most repulsive gods, the limping Hephaestus. Hera was the mother of

Hephaestus and hence her mother-in-law. But she had no true parents of her own. She had been born on the foaming crest of a wave, carried across the sea by the West Wind and thrown, perfectly formed, onto the coast of Cyprus.

Now she stood naked before Paris and laughed at his discomfort.

"To the fairest," she began. "Already I think you have made up your mind, shepherd-boy. I can see it by the blush in your young cheeks, the way you try to avoid my eyes. Well, Paris, if you are as wise as you are handsome – and you are very handsome – you will know what to do with this precious golden apple.

"You have been offered . . . this and that. Money, power, strength – mere bribes, and nothing to do with man's greatest pleasure. I think I can offer you something a little more . . . stimulating. How would you like to find yourself married to Helen?"

"Helen?" His mouth was dry.

"Yes. Helen of Sparta. I dare say you know her name."

"Is she as beautiful as the stories say?" Paris asked.

"More beautiful."

"But she is married . . ."

"That can be dealt with."

"You promise?"

"I promise."

"Then the apple is yours!"

Paris gestured and Hermes, who had been watching the contest in silence, stepped forward to give the prize to the winner. The apple seemed light in Aphrodite's hand and she held it as if she had never really wanted it in the first place. But Hera and Athene trembled with anger. While Aphrodite laughed, they gathered up their clothes and disappeared from Mount Gargarus to suffer their bitterness in solitude, consoling themselves with thoughts of revenge.

But all Paris could think of was the prize he had won by his judgement.

"Tell me about Helen," he demanded. "Many travellers have spoken of her. They say she is the most beautiful woman who ever lived. Is it true?"

"She is even more beautiful than I am," Aphrodite said.

And with a smile that hid a dark and dangerous knowledge, she told him about the woman whose beauty was soon to cause the dreadful war of Troy.

### Helen

"Amongst the many loves of Zeus there was a mortal woman, Leda by name, the wife of a certain King Tyndareus. Love? Zeus could have become the god of love himself so healthy an interest did he take in its pleasures. Well, he knew that Leda was not for him. She was devoted to her husband for a start. And she would hardly let herself be seduced by a man old enough to be her father!

"And so he tricked her. One day, as she sat beside the River Eurotas, a white swan appeared, gliding silently towards her. How happy she was to see it, its feathers radiant in the sunlight! How she laughed as the swan brushed her bare legs with its wings. But the swan (of course you have guessed) was Zeus in disguise and while Leda was off her guard, he suddenly pounced. She struggled, but it was too late. From this brief encounter a child was born, a daughter whom she called Helen.

"How can I describe how lovely that young girl was, how talented, how charming? Suffice it to say that when she was barely ten years old, she was carried off by none other than Theseus himself. The slayer of the Minotaur would gladly have made her his wife had not her two half-brothers arrived in the nick of time to carry her home. By the time she had reached the marrying age, her father's palace was filled to the brim with some of the finest young men in Greece, all of them as neatly pierced with Cupid's arrows as you could wish. Who was there? Well, Ajax was one of them. Today he is one of the most admired warriors in the country. Then there was Patroclus, the cousin of Achilles, and . . . well, Helen was always surrounded by men and there were so many of them you never knew who exactly was there.

"In fact, her father, Tyndareus, became quite worried by the situation. He was afraid that once he announced the name of the lucky man, he would have a riot on his hands. And so it might have been, had he not forced all of them to swear a sacred oath that no matter who was chosen as Helen's husband, they would always come to his aid when he was in need. They swore, and when Prince Menelaus was named (he now rules as King of Sparta) they could do nothing but congratulate him, albeit rather grudgingly.

"They have been married now for three years, and very happily by all accounts. Why then, you may be wondering, should Helen want to leave him and run away with you? The answer to that, my dear Paris, is simple. When Tyndareus married Leda – this was long before her encounter with Zeus – he naturally made sacrifices to all the gods, as is the custom. Unfortunately, the foolish man left out one of the more important goddesses who swore that his children would be notorious for their adulteries. So you see, the marriage of Helen was doomed from the start. She was born an adulteress, and an adulteress she shall be."

This was what Aphrodite told the shepherd. What she did not tell him was that it was she who had been forgotten at the wedding of Tyndareus. And by arranging Helen's flight with Paris, she was not only paying the price for the golden apple. She was repaying a slight and fulfilling an ancient curse.

### Troy

Shortly after the judgement, Paris decided to attend the annual games held in the city of Troy. Here he was recognized by his father, King Priam, and welcomed back into the palace. No longer a shepherd but a prince, he sailed to Sparta where he cynically took advantage of the king's hospitality to steal away with his wife. Although the jealous Hera sent a storm to try to stop them, Paris and Helen sailed safely back to Troy. The Trojan people fell in love with the Greek queen the moment they saw her. Soon she delivered three sons: Bunomus, Aganis and Idaeus. For a time, they were happy.

But Paris had been deceived by Aphrodite and had underestimated the wrath of Menelaus. The King of Sparta was enraged not only by the theft of his wife but by the underhand method in which it had been accomplished — while Paris was a guest in his own house. Helped by his brother Agamemnon, he set about raising an army the size of which had never been seen nor even dreamt of before. He began with all the kings and princes who had once been the suitors of Helen, the same men who had sworn to come to his aid. To these he added just about every great warrior alive: Odysseus, Achilles (the son of Peleus and Thetis), Nestor, Diomedes . . . and many more.

They came to Aulis, a secluded beach in the Euboean straits. Soon there were so many men lining the shore that you could no longer see the sand. The fleet, stretching as far as the horizon, was like an incredible floating city. After sacrificing to Zeus and Apollo, the fleet departed, slowly sailing into a sun that was as cruel as the sacrificial flames.

They would not return until the great city of Troy was utterly destroyed, its sons killed and maimed, its daughters sold as slaves. This was the legacy that Paris brought his countrymen. This was the fate that his mother had once foretold.

Virtually all the men and women who have played a part

in this story were to die. Not one single person would escape his share of suffering. And seventeen years would pass before Menelaus and Helen were reunited.

The marriage of Peleus would soon collapse. All his children would die, Achilles falling with a poisoned arrow in his heel. King Priam too would see the corpses of many of his children before he was himself slaughtered on the altar of his palace. Captivity in Greece awaited Queen Hecuba. She would finally be transformed into a dog, baying at the moon in her madness and grief. Ajax, Patroclus, Agamemnon, the three sons of Paris ... and Paris himself. They would all die.

And what of the gods and goddesses with whom the story began? Although they would watch over the battlefield, over the growing pools of blood; although they would sometimes help one side, sometimes the other, they would not die. For they were immortal. They would not even suffer.

*As flies to wanton boys, are we to the gods;*
*They kill us for their sport.*

(William Shakespeare, *King Lear*)

# THE SEVEN POMEGRANATE SEEDS
GREEK

Demeter was one of the more gentle goddesses who inhabited Mount Olympus. Not for her were the jealous rages of Hera, the whip-like chastity of Artemis or the burning passions of Aphrodite. Demeter was the goddess of agriculture and of marriage. Her hair was the colour of wheat at harvest-time and her eyes were a pastel blue. She delighted in bright colours, often wearing brilliant ribbons and carrying a golden torch.

Only once did she really lose her temper. This was when she discovered that the beautiful trees in a grove that was sacred to her were being cut down by a foolhardy young man called Erysichthon. Perhaps he was some sort of early town planner, but whatever his reason for this act of vandalism, Demeter appeared to him disguised as a mortal and asked him if he would be so kind as to stop. His answer was short and unfriendly.

Then Demeter assumed her own form and punished Erysichthon in a way that was truly horrible. She condemned him to remain hungry for ever, no matter how much he ate. From that moment on, he seldom stopped. At dinner that same night, he astonished his parents by eating not only his food but theirs too – as well as that of their seventeen guests. In the weeks that followed, he ate so much that his weeping father was forced to throw him out of the house, no longer able to afford his keep. And yet the more he ate, the thinner and hungrier he got until, in the end, he became a beggar, shuffling pathetically along in rags, still stuffing himself with the filth he found in the streets.

This, then, was the full extent of Demeter's anger. But most people would agree that Erysichthon only got what he deserved. For the unnecessary destruction of a tree is a terrible crime.

Demeter had a daughter called Core (later on, her name was changed to Persephone) whom she loved more than anything in the world. Unfortunately, another of the gods also loved the girl, although in a very different way. This was Hades, the shadowy lord of the Underworld, the god of death. Hades had spent virtually his whole life underground and his skin was pale and cold. No light shone in his eyes, eyes that had seldom seen the sun. And yet he had seen an image of Core, magically reflected in an ebony pool, and he had lost his heart to her. So great was his love that he took a rare leave of absence from the Underworld, travelling to Olympus. There he came before Zeus and demanded that he give Core to him as a wife.

The demand somewhat embarrassed the king of the gods. For although he did not want to offend Hades, who was his brother, Zeus could not let him have what he wanted. For Core was his daughter. He had fallen in love with Demeter some years before and Core had been the result. If he were to send the girl to the Underworld, Demeter would never forgive him. Moreover, it would hardly be fair to condemn his own daughter to such a gloomy place – for the kingdom of Hades was such a dull and dismal land. But on the other hand, what was he to say to Hades, who was older than he and . . . ?

"I'll think about it," Zeus said.

And promptly forgot all about it.

When it became clear that he was not going to get a satisfactory answer out of Zeus, Hades decided to take things into his own hands.

"He did not say I could have the girl," he reasoned to himself. "But nor did he say that I could not. And surely, if something is not forbidden, then it must be allowed. Of course it must! In which case, Core shall become Persephone and as Persephone she will be my wife."

And so it was that two days later, Core found herself kidnapped by the grim god of death. She was living in Sicily at the time and was out in the fields with some of her friends, collecting wild flowers for a feast that same evening. Noticing a particularly bright narcissus, she leant down to pick it. Suddenly the ground trembled. As the blood drained from her face and her friends screamed, dropping their baskets and scattering in all directions, a great chasm appeared in front of her, yawning like a black mouth. Desperately, Core tried to keep her balance. But then a white hand that smelt of damp earth stretched out and grabbed hold of her, pulling her forward. With a hopeless cry, she tumbled forward, disappearing into the chasm. The ground trembled again, then closed up as suddenly as it had opened. Only a jagged line, zig-zagging through the flowers, showed what had happened.

When Demeter discovered that Core was missing, her grief was overwhelming. Almost overnight she changed. No longer did she wear ribbons and bright colours. No more was her laughter heard in the fields. Covering herself with a dark veil, she flew round the world on a search that would take her nine days and nine nights. Not once did she stop for food or for drink – nor even to rest. Her only thought was for her daughter. She visited Sicily, Colonus, Hermione, Crete, Pisa, Lerna . . . nobody had seen the girl, nor was there any sign that she had been there.

At last she went in desperation to Helios, the god who every day followed the sun, riding across the heavens in a golden chariot drawn by four white horses. Nothing ever escaped the eye of Helios. Soaring in an arc, high above the world, he could see everything. And what he had to tell Demeter chilled her heart.

"You must forget Core," he said. "Core exists no longer. Look, if you will, for Persephone – destroyer of men – for that is what she has become as wife of the king of death. Yes! Hades has stolen her from you. Never again will you see her. Where she is now, deep in the shadows of the Underworld, she is lost even from the sight of Helios."

At once Demeter went to Zeus. White with anger and haggard after her nine days of fasting, she was almost unrecognizable and the king of the gods squirmed in front of her.

"I didn't say Hades could take her," he muttered.

"Did you say he couldn't?"

"Well . . ."

"I want her back, Zeus. You will return her to me!"

"I can't!" The king of the gods almost wept with frustration. "You know the rules. If she has eaten so much as a mouthful of the food of the dead, she is stuck in the Underworld for ever."

"She won't have eaten. She can't have eaten."

"And anyway," Zeus went on, "you know Hades. There's no arguing with him. He has to have his own way . . ."

"Very well," Demeter cried. "Until my daughter is returned to me, no tree on earth will yield fruit. No plants will grow. The soil will remain barren. The animals will starve. Such is the curse of an unhappy mother. Bring her back, Zeus. Or mankind will perish!"

So began a year of unrelenting famine. The crops withered and even the grass turned brown and rotted. As Demeter had promised, the animals, unable to find fodder, died by the hundred, their bloated carcasses dotting the arid landscape.

At last the situation became so desperate that Hermes, the messenger-god, was sent down to the Underworld to bring Persephone back.

"Never!" Hades exclaimed. "I love her. I will never relinquish her."

"But does she love you?" Hermes asked.

"She . . . she will learn to. In time."

"But there is no time," Hermes said. "Her mother, Demeter, is destroying the world in her grief. If you do not release Persephone, mankind will come to an end."

"Why should the extinction of mankind be of any concern to the god of death?" Hades asked.

"Because even death depends on life. Nothing can continue without it."

The king of the Underworld thought long and hard but then he nodded his head.

"You speak the truth," he said. "Very well. It seems that I am defeated. My wife, my Persephone . . . she must go."

And he turned his head, bringing his hand up to cover his eyes.

When Persephone heard that she was to be returned to the world of the living, she was so happy that she laughed and cried at the same time. But one of the gardeners of Hades, a man by the name of Ascalaphus, also heard the news and at once he crept off and, changing into his best clothes, knelt before Hades.

"Oh ghastly and glorious master!" he said, rubbing his hands together in front of his chin. "Dread lord of the Underworld, grotesque king of the dead, sovereign of the . . . "

"Get on with it!" Hades commanded.

"Of course! Of course!" The gardener laughed nervously. "I just thought you'd like to know that your wife, the good and delicious lady Persephone, has tasted the food of the dead."

"That's impossible," Hades said. "She has refused to eat since the day I brought her here. Not so much as a crust of bread has passed her lips."

"I'm sure. I'm sure. But something less than a crust of bread has, noble king. With my own eyes I saw her eat seven pomegranate seeds. In the garden. I saw her."

Then the eyes of Hades lit up. "If this is true," he said, "you shall be rewarded."

"Rewarded?" Ascalaphus licked his lips. "Well, I didn't do it for the reward. But if there is a reward. Well . . ."

"Follow her to the surface," Hades said. "Do what must be done."

So when Hermes took Persephone with him in his chariot, Ascalaphus rode on the back, unseen by either of them, dreaming of his new career (for he had never liked gardening very much), perhaps as secretary to Hades or perhaps as palace librarian or even – who could say? – as the next prince of Hell. And no sooner had Demeter received her daughter in a joyful embrace than he stepped forward with a crooked smile.

"Persephone has eaten the food of the dead," he cried. "She must return with me to the Underworld. There's nothing any of you lot can do about it. It's the law."

"Is this true?" Demeter asked.

Then tears sprang to Persephone's eyes and she sank to her knees.

"Yes, Mother," she whispered. "I ate seven pomegranate seeds. But that was all I ate. Although I was one year in that horrible place, that was the only food that passed my lips. Surely it doesn't count. Surely . . ."

But by now Demeter was weeping too.

"You have eaten the food of the dead," she said. "Though mankind will die when they take you from me, there is nothing I can do."

When the gods heard what had happened, they held a great conference to discuss what should be done. On the one hand, nobody wanted the world to end. But nor could they allow Persephone to remain in the land of the living. At last, a compromise was reached and both Persephone and Demeter were called before the throne of Zeus.

"We've come to an agreement," Zeus explained. "And I hope it satisfies you because it really is the best we can do. Listen. What would you say if we allowed Persephone to stay in the world for six months of the year, provided she spent the other six months with Hades in the Underworld?"

Demeter thought for a moment. "Make it nine months with me and three months with Hades and I will agree," she said.

"Very well. You've got a deal."

At once the famine ended. Nine months later, Persephone went back to begin her spell in the Underworld, and although she was never a truly loving wife to Hades, she was never unkind to him.

The miserable Ascalaphus never received the reward he had been hoping for. For Persephone punished him for his treachery by pushing him into a small hole and covering him with an ornamental rockery complete with flowering hibiscus border and fish-pond. In this way he was condemned to spend the rest of eternity not only in the garden but under it too.

This myth explains why it is that for three months every year, the cold season comes and it looks as though the world has gone into mourning. Then the trees lose their leaves, nothing will grow and, like Demeter, we look forward to the spring. For it is only in the spring, when Persephone is released from her dark confinement, that the warmth and the colours will return and we can all − god and man − celebrate the return of life.

# THE SPINNING CONTEST
## GREEK

In Ancient Greece, it was always considered a wise move to thank the gods for a particular skill or talent that you happened to possess. If you really admired someone, you might go so far as to compare him to the gods. "He sings almost like Apollo," you might say – and you would be careful not to forget the "almost". But were you to claim that you did something as well as or even better than the gods . . . well, that could be very dangerous. In fact it could be lethal.

This is the story of just such a person, a girl by the name of Arachne. She was a young woman of Maeonia. Her family was poor and she had been born in a tiny cottage in the somewhat decrepit village of Hypaepae. Hypaepae was such a wretched place that the only people who visited invariably turned out to have lost their way and those who lived in it would really have preferred not to. Hypaepae didn't have a village green. It had a village mouldy brown. Although it seldom rained, the high street was always full of puddles and the whole place smelt of fish.

Despite this inauspicious beginning, Arachne soon became famous throughout the country on account of her extraordinary skill at weaving. Then people did start coming to the village, just to admire her work – and it wasn't only the finished product that made it worth the journey. To watch her weave, her fingers dancing over the pattern, was a pleasure in itself. There was an extraordinary elegance in the way she wound yarn. To see her draw a single soft thread out of a great ball of fluff was like watching a conjuror. Whether she was twirling the spindle with a single flick of her thumb or embroidering the finished material, nobody could take their eyes off her.

You may think that this is all a little exaggerated, but watch any craftsman at work and you will see for yourself. A potter "growing" a vase between his fingers, a glass-blower forming crystal bubbles over the flames, a carpenter stroking virgin wood with his chisel . . . there is a type of magic in craftsmanship and Arachne had plenty of it.

Unfortunately, she was somewhat less well endowed with the virtues of modesty, humility and generosity. It is often the way that people who are particularly good at something are a little short on human kindness. Arachne had none at all. She was rude to her mother, quick-tempered with her servants and generally difficult and unfriendly. But it was her arrogance that eventually undid her.

"I am so unbelievably, unusually and extraordinarily talented," she remarked one day to her mother.

"Yes, dear," her mother said, stifling a yawn. She had heard it all before.

"Even the gods must envy me," she continued.

"Well, dear, I'm not so sure . . . "

"No god can weave as I can. Not even Athene. Compared to me, the so-called goddess of wisdom is just a clodhopper, a fat-fingered fumbler. I bet she's jealous of me. Everybody's jealous of me. But then I'd be jealous of me if I wasn't me. Because I'm so extravagantly talented."

Now this was a doubly foolish thing to say. For Athene was the goddess who had taught Arachne her skill in the first place. And secondly, she tended to react rather severely to insults such as these. In her twin-role as goddess of war, she had once crushed one of her enemies to death using the entire island of Sicily. Her curses had caused one man to be flayed alive and another – the prophet Tiresias – to go blind. Athene was a kind and caring friend. But she was a terrible enemy.

But Arachne went on regardless.

"I bet Athene would never compete against me," she said. "She'd be too afraid of losing, especially against a supposed mortal. But then, perhaps there is a little goddess in me. What do you think? Don't you think I'm just a teeny-weeny bit divine?"

These words were no sooner out of her mouth than an old woman, who had somehow got into the room without anyone hearing her, stepped forward, supporting herself on a gnarled walking stick. She really was very old. Her hair was quite white, her skin hanging in bags and her eyes dim and blistered.

"Ugh!" Arachne exclaimed. "Who are you, old crone?"

"You shouldn't mock old age," the woman said. "For with it comes experience. Listen now to the voice of experience, Arachne. It is all very well to consider yourself the best mortal spinner. Perhaps you are. But you are wrong to compare yourself to the goddess Athene and should ask her pardon."

"Why should I?"

"Because she will forgive you if you ask. If you do not, who can say what she will do?"

Arachne scowled. She had been weaving when she was interrupted, but now she stopped, got up and roughly pushed the old woman against the wall.

"You know what your trouble is?" she said. "You're old. You're senile. Your brains have gone. You're like my mother. Don't you have daughters of your own to go and nag? Because don't imagine for a single minute that I care what you say. If Athene was so clever, she'd have come here herself. And even then I wouldn't apologise. I'd weave – and I can tell you, I'd show her a thing or two."

"Very well," the old woman said. "Now is your opportunity."

And suddenly she raised her arm, there was a burst of light and in an instant she was transformed. Gone were the old clothes, the walking-stick, the wrinkles. In their place stood a tall, armoured woman carrying a spear in one hand and a shield in the other. A helmet with five spikes surmounted her head and sheer power seemed to radiate around her.

"You have challenged me," Athene said, for of course it was the goddess herself. "And I have come. Soon you may regret it."

When the transformation had taken place, many of the women in the room had fled, screaming with fear. But Arachne just smiled.

"I don't regret anything!"

And so, while her mother watched, tight-lipped and pale, two looms were set up on opposite sides of the room. The goddess sat at one, the mortal at the other, back-to-back so that neither could see what the other was doing.

"Speed must count as well as technique," Athene said. "We will stop at sunset. Then we can compare what we have done."

"I'm ready when you are," Arachne said.

"Then we will start."

It was the strangest race that was ever run. First the contestants stretched the threads on their looms. They tied their frames to the crossbeams, separated the warp with their heddles, reached for their shuttles to weave the crossthreads . . . in this way an expert might have described it. But to the onlookers, unskilled in the art of weaving, it was as if the two figures were playing incredibly complicated, multi-stringed instruments without actually managing to make a single sound. For they worked in silence, their fingers racing back and forth across the frames, plucking and pulling, dipping in and out of the threads, pulling, separating, weaving . . .

And gradually two pictures began to form. First there would be one colour. Then another. Then a line of gold. A shape. A hand . . . then an arm. The hands continue their mad pattern and a man springs to life, posing against a background of Tyrian copper. A man? No. The threads have been beaten back by the comb and he has metamorphosed. Below the waist he is a horse. Of course! A Centaur . . .

This is what the two contestants wove that day:

Arachne wove a tapestry called "The Loves of the Gods". It depicted Zeus no less than three times but always in different guises: as a bull, seducing Europa, as a swan in the arms of Leda and as a shower of gold coins, tumbling into the lap of Danae. But Zeus was not the only god whose wickedness she portrayed. There was Poseidon as a bull, as a ram and as a river – always as an adulterer. There was Apollo, disguised as a humble shepherd to deceive the simple country-girl, Isse. And there was even the drunken god of wine, Bacchus, who had turned himself into a bunch of grapes in order to hang at the lips of the woman he loved. The tapestry was formed out of dozens of radiant colours. It was gaily decorated with a framework of flowers and ivy. But still it showed the gods at their most ignoble.

The theme of Athene's tapestry was very different, for it was as flattering as Arachne's was irreverent. Here again was Zeus, but this time he was revealed in his full glory as king of Olympus, a thunder-bolt in his hand and an eagle perched behind his throne. Poseidon stood with his trident, striking a rock to release a sparkling waterfall. Athene herself appeared in her own tapestry, creating a mighty olive tree simply by touching the ground with her spear. The tapestry was called "The Power of the Gods".

But in each of the four corners of her work, the goddess added different scenes: scenes that would have warned Arachne of her terrible danger had she only been able to see it. For they showed punishments that the gods had inflicted on mortals unwise enough to fall into their disfavour. There was Rhodope, changed into an icy mountain. Antigone and the queen of the pygmies both turned into birds. And Cinyras shedding bitter tears on the limbs of his dead daughters. Athene finished her work by embroidering the edges with olives, the symbols of peace.

The sun set and the contest ended. At last the two opponents stopped and turned round to face each other. Arachne's back was stiff and her fingers were sore and bleeding, but Athene was as fresh as when she had started.

"Now let us compare our work," Athene said.

Coldly, she ran her eye over "The Loves of the Gods".

"Hardly the way a mortal should represent the Olympians," she remarked. "But . . . " She pursed her lips. "The work is perfect."

"Of course it is," Arachne said, smugly.

"It is. It's . . . "

"It's better than yours."

Then the goddess of wisdom and of war became angry because, astonished and disgusted though she was, she could not deny that Arachne was right. The mortal woman had beaten her at her own craft. Seeing Athene so indignant, Arachne broke into laughter, the shrill sound echoing round the room. But her mother trembled, seeing the blood run from Athene's face.

"Better than yours! Better than yours!" Arachne shouted.

"Enough!" the goddess cried.

Raising her shuttle, she struck Arachne hard on the forehead, then again and again and again. Arachne screamed and fell to the floor. But the goddess had not finished yet. Forming a noose out of thread, she slipped it round Arachne's neck and while the wretched girl gurgled and grunted, drew it tight, pulling her off her feet so that she hung beneath the rafters.

It was then, seeing her daughter slowly strangle, that Arachne's mother threw herself forward, kneeling at the feet of the goddess.

"Great Athene!" she cried. "Forgive my little girl. She didn't know what she was doing. She doesn't mean to offend. It's just . . . well, she's a nasty piece of work . . . I admit it. But you can't kill her. I beg you . . . !"

Then Athene's heart softened. Regarding her foolish opponent who was now bright red, swaying like a pendulum in the air some six feet above the ground, she sprinkled her with a handful of herbs which had been prepared by the witch, Hecate.

"I will spare your life, wretch!" she said. "But this is how you must remain for all eternity. And this is how all your daughters shall be. Such is the punishment for your insolence and vanity."

The moment the poisoned herbs touched Arachne, all her hair fell out, immediately followed by her nose and ears.

While her mother fainted dead away, Arachne's head shrank like a punctured balloon until it was no bigger than a pea. At the same time, her body folded in on itself, trapping her legs and arms which disappeared completely. Her fingers, which had scuttled so quickly across the threads, became stuck to her sides to serve her as legs. But they were thinner now, and hairy too.

And just as Athene had ordained, that was how Arachne remained. She still hung above the ground. And she still wove beautifully – although in not quite the same way.

For Arachne had been turned into a spider.

# THE STORY OF THE PAN-PIPES
## GREEK

Zeus, the king of the Greek gods, argued frequently with his wife, Hera. Many of these arguments were about young women, of whom Zeus was particularly fond. Unfortunately, it was often this these young women who came off the worst from the arguments. Take the case of Io, for example. No sooner had Zeus fallen in love with her than he was forced to change her into a white heifer (a young cow) to keep her out of Hera's sight. But then Hera discovered the trick, captured Io and locked her up in a gloomy cave where she was guarded by a monster called Argus. Argus was well suited to the task because he had no less than one hundred eyes. No matter how long or how heavily he slept, at least two of these eyes would always remain open – so poor Io could never escape.

Eventually Zeus decided that Io had suffered enough and sent Hermes, the messenger of the gods, to kill Argus and rescue her. But Hermes had a problem. There was no angle from which he could sneak up on Argus without being spotted, no way that he could take him by surprise. So instead he thought up a plan. He walked up to the cave quite boldly playing a set of pan-pipes and the sound of his music delighted Argus so much that the monster became quite friendly.

"Tell me, stranger," he growled (even when he was being friendly he still growled, so you can imagine what he was like when he was angry), "what is the instrument that you play so skilfully?"

"Why, sir," Hermes replied. "This is a set of pan-pipes."

"Pan-pipes?" Argus repeated. "What a strange name! Would I be right in thinking they have something to do with frying-pans?"

"Not exactly," Hermes said, wondering why so many monsters were quite so stupid. "As a matter of fact, they're named after my son."

"Your son? Clever boy! Tell me about him."

"With pleasure, sir."

Hermes sat down on the grass in front of the cave, stretching out his winged feet and laying his sword down beside him. It was a warm and sunny day and already Argus was feeling drowsy. No less than fifteen of his hundred eyes had closed. *Eighty-five to go,* Hermes thought to himself. Then, with a smile, he began the story of the pan-pipes. And this is how it went:

"Pan was the god of shepherds and of herds. He lived on the slopes of Mount Maenalus where the Arcadian shepherds came to worship him. For he was also the god of fertility and of growth. When you prayed to Pan, you knew that your flock was sure to increase.

"He was a strange fellow to look at. He was shaped like a man only as far down as the waist. Beneath that he was shaped like a goat with hairy legs, a tail and hooves. He also had goat's ears although he partly concealed these under a wreath of pine leaves. Whatever his appearance, though, you couldn't help liking him. He was always laughing and singing and dancing. He was very partial to wine and frequently drank too much. Pan really *was* the merriest of gods. Only in the afternoon, when the sun was at its hottest, did he like to find a lonely and sheltered place where he could sleep in peace. To have woken him up at that time would have been a great mistake for his voice was so loud that it could turn a man's hair white, and if he was in a really bad mood he would send you nightmares that would keep you awake for weeks."

Argus was not enjoying the story very much. It had begun promisingly, but there had been altogether too much description. *If only the stranger would use fewer adjectives,* he thought, *I might enjoy it a bit more.* As it was, another twenty-seven of his eyes closed in sleep.

"Pan was also a very lusty god. Nothing pleased him more than to chase girls across the fields until they were too exhausted to run any more. The girls, for their part, would scream when they saw him coming but secretly they were rather flattered by his attentions and made quite sure that they didn't run too fast.

"There was, however, one exception. Her name was Syrinx and she was a nymph, the most beautiful nymph Pan had ever seen. She had long fair hair, pale skin, deep brown eyes and a wonderfully slender body. The colour in her cheeks was that of the sun on a spring morning."

*Why doesn't he get to the point?* Argus thought to himself. Another twenty-four eyes closed. That made sixty-six in all.

"Now Syrinx was a huntress and a worshipper of Artemis. Artemis was, as you may know, the goddess of the hunt and the moon and all nature. She was by nature strict and did not encourage casual affairs between young men and women. Syrinx worshipped Artemis so much that she even looked like her. Indeed she had often been mistaken for her when wearing her hunting dress and running barefoot through the woods. The only obvious difference between them was that Syrinx carried a bow made of horn whereas that of Artemis was made of gold. Anyway, having spent her life avoiding the company of men, you can imagine how Syrinx felt when she found herself pursued by a grinning half-man, half-goat.

"She screamed and ran. How she ran! She didn't stop for six hours. How many animals had run from her in just the same way as she now ran from Pan, crashing through the undergrowth, sobbing with each breath?

"Pan wouldn't give up. All his other conquests were forgotten as he raced after the nymph. She was lovely. She was enchanting. She was fast! He thought that he would never catch her, but then he saw her slow down and stumble to a halt. A wide river ran through the forest – the River Ladon – and she had reached its edge. She could go no further. Pan laughed with excitement. He had her! The river was flowing too fast for her to be able to swim across. There was nowhere else to run. She was his!"

But Argus didn't care. Seventeen more eyes closed. Like so many monsters, he just didn't have the time for stories . . .

"Syrinx, finding herself trapped, raised her arms and called out to the nymphs who inhabited the waters of the river to protect her. And her sisters heard her. Pan rushed forwards, but he was too late. Just when he thought he had her in his arms, he found that she was gone and all that remained was a handful of marsh reeds.

"He stood there beside the river, sighing to himself. But then, as he turned to leave, the wind blew through the reeds, making a strange, sad sound – almost like music. Hearing it, the smile returned to Pan's face and he turned back.

"'Syrinx!' he exclaimed. 'You may have escaped me, but together we can still make music.'

"And so saying, he leant down and cut reeds of different lengths and fastened them together with wax. This was how the first pan-pipe was made. And pan-pipes are still played to this very day."

Argus was no longer listening. His last two eyes had closed. All one hundred of them were shut. It was what Hermes had been waiting for. Gently, he lifted his sword, then brought it whistling through the air. The monster's head parted company with his shoulders and his body rolled away down the hill. Then Hermes went into the cave and although Io's troubles were far from over, at least she was delivered from her prison.

Hera, when she saw what had happened to her servant, took his eyes and used them to decorate the feathers of her favourite bird. The next time you see a peacock spread its tail, look closely. You will have seen the hundred eyes of Argus.

# GLAUCUS AND SCYLLA
## GREEK

There was, at a place called Anthedon, opposite Euboea, a secluded beach where the white sand formed a perfect crescent between the meadows and the sea. Although the fishermen who inhabited that part of the country sailed their ships up and down the coast, none had ever stepped onto that beach. For even from a distance they could feel that there was something strange about it . . . something not quite right.

It was nothing you could pin down. Perhaps the breeze was a little too still, the colours a little too intense. Perhaps the waves that broke against the sand seemed to pull back a little too quickly. It was certainly true that the animals, who can sense things no man ever can, avoided the place. No cattle or sheep grazed in the meadows. Even the bees passed over the flowers. At the end of the day, there was nothing you could put your finger on. But enchantment has its own peculiar smell and the beach at Anthedon stank of it.

But one evening, a fisherman returning home anchored his boat and came ashore to count the fish he had taken in his nets that day. His name was Glaucus, a young, cheerful man who feared nothing. He was in a good mood. It had been a hard day's work but, laying his fish in the sand, he could see that it was an excellent catch. Half a dozen snappers, twice as many mullet and a prime swordfish lay stretched out in front of him.

A movement caught his eye. Was it his imagination or

had the tail of the swordfish twitched? He blinked, then shook his head. The fish had been out of the water for an hour. It was impossible. It . . .

It twitched again. Then a couple of mullet flipped over. He looked more closely at his catch. All the fish had miraculously returned to life. Even as he sat there, with a reed that he had plucked from the beach clasped between his teeth, the fish began to wriggle back to the sea. He was too surprised to stop them. Often he had been told that Anthedon was enchanted. Now that he saw it with his own eyes, he was more astonished than afraid. Only when the last fish had disappeared into the sea and he realised that he had lost his entire catch did he grit his teeth in vexation, breaking the reed.

Sap squirted into his mouth. He felt it on his tongue, tasting of honey. Before he could stop himself, he had swallowed it.

"Great heavens . . . !" he muttered.

His heart began to beat faster and faster. It felt as if his clothes were squeezing him to death and with scrabbling fingers he tore them off until he stood naked on the beach. But now the sand burnt his feet and the sun, though low in the sky, beat down on him. He turned and looked at the sea. How inviting the water was! How he longed to lose himself in its cool embrace. Despite his discomfort, he couldn't help laughing.

"Goodbye, world!" he cried. "You and I must part company."

Then he dived into the water, leaving his boat and his clothes to tell their own story.

Glaucus did not drown. As he sank further and further away from the air and the sun, he found (and it was a very agreeable surprise) that he could breathe. And, strangely, he felt at one with the element. It was like flying. He wasn't exactly wet as he would never again be exactly dry. The surface of the ocean was his sky, the sea-bed his land and he somersaulted between them, silent bubbles of laughter erupting from his mouth. He felt like a different man.

And a different man was just what he was. For the sap had transformed him in more ways than one. His beard, once light brown, was now a rusty green. His hair had more than doubled in length, flowing over shoulders that were suddenly much broader than they had ever been on land. His arms were dark blue. More peculiar than all these metamorphoses put together, his legs had somehow become fused as one, becoming a fish's tail just around where the hips should have been. But a fish's tail was certainly a great deal more useful than two ungainly feet – as Glaucus soon found out. The merest flick could propel him at speed along the sea-bed and by twisting it he could dodge the coral and zig-zag through the dunes.

So began his life under the sea. In the weeks that followed, he was introduced to the sea-gods Oceanus and Tethys who welcomed him to their world. He rode on the backs of dolphins, revelling in their laughter as they raced across the surface of the sea. He discovered caves lit by phosphorescent stone where fish more beautiful than he had ever seen hid from the nets of the fishermen. He met the Oceanids, the three thousand nymphs of the oceans, and joined in their feasting. And he fell in love with Scylla.

Scylla was a Nereid, one of the nymphs of the sea who come to the aid of sailors in distress. She was the loveliest creature he had ever seen either in the water or on land. He came upon her in a sunlit grotto where she was sitting on a rock, combing her long fair hair. Although her shape was that of a human, she was no larger than a young girl. Her eyes were of a colour caught somewhere between hazel and green. Her lips were full, her whole body lithe and graceful.

Glaucus swam towards her, then lay where the water was at its most shallow, propping himself against a rock. She saw him. He smiled. She screamed and dropped her comb.

"What . . . monster are you?" she cried.

"Monster?" Glaucus scratched his head indignantly. "I'm no monster, lady. My name is Glaucus. Don't let these blue arms of mine and all the rest of it put you off. Once I was a mortal . . . a fisherman (although in the circumstances, I tend not to mention it). Now I'm a sort of . . . merman, and the sea is my home. The gods themselves have made me welcome – and may the gods bless them for it. Now, the thing is, I couldn't help noticing you sitting here, and the thing is, well . . . I was wondering, you see, if . . . "

Glaucus had gone very red but even as he spoke, Scylla had turned her back on him and run off into the forest.

Then for the first time in a long time Glaucus was sad.

He could not understand why Scylla should have rejected him so cruelly, even if his advances had been somewhat inept. What he did not know was that Scylla, rejoicing rather too much in her own beauty, rejected everybody. She had not yet found a man good enough for her in her own eyes and she did not care how she let her admirers know it.

But Glaucus was not to be put off so easily. He had seen her only once but he knew that he could never forget her nor rest until she had accepted him. Now he turned and swam to the island of Aeaea. For he had heard tell of a powerful sorceress called Circe who lived there. And he needed her help.

This was the same Circe whom Odysseus would one day encounter on his wanderings after the Trojan War. The daughter of the sun-god, Helios, she was a proud and mysterious goddess, skilled in every type of magic, but never to be trusted. She lived in a palace in the middle of a thick forest of oak trees where wolves and lions prowled – and not all of them had begun their lives as animals. For Circe delighted in feeding her guests potions that might turn them into a wolf or a lion . . . or something worse.

Glaucus came to her as she sat on the shore of her island, her eyes on the horizon, dreaming of secret things.

"Great Circe!" he cried. "I am only a humble man . . . well not exactly a man, as you can see, but humble all the same. I come to you for help. I know you're busy! But it won't take long . . . that is, if you agree to help."

Then Circe smiled. For Glaucus's looks pleased her as

did his rough and awkward manner. "Speak on, little sea-creature," she said. "What can I do for you?"

"Well, it's like this, your majesty. I'm in love with a Nereid, but the thing is, she isn't exactly mad about me. Now, what I was hoping was that you could fix me up with some sort of potion . . . you know . . . magic herbs or something . . . "

"You want me to cure you of your love?" Circe interrupted.

"No! No! That's the last thing I want. No! It's for her. I want her to fall in love with me."

Circe looked at Glaucus thoughtfully.

"If, as you say, this Nereid has rejected you," she said, "then perhaps you should forget her. Would it not be more sensible to search for a woman who loves you as much as you might learn to love her? Someone like myself, for example. I may be a goddess, but I live alone on this island. There is much I could offer you if you were to . . . "

"Oh no!" Glaucus burst in. "Begging your pardon, your highness, but that wouldn't do at all. I mean . . . no offence. But really . . . !"

"You should forget this Nereid of yours," Circe snapped angrily.

"I can't!" Glaucus replied. "Leaves will grow in the sea and seaweed on the mountain tops before my feelings for Scylla change."

"Very well!" Circe said and if Glaucus had been looking more carefully, he would have seen two flames suddenly smoulder in her eyes. "I will prepare you a potion that will change your Scylla . . . "

"You will?" Glaucus exclaimed in delight.

"Oh yes. It will change her. Wait for me here."

And with these enigmatic words, Circe swept away, disappearing into the darkness of the forest.

She returned an hour later, carrying a small leather bag.

"Take the contents of this pouch," she said, "and sprinkle them in the water where your Scylla likes to swim. Inside there are certain roots over which I have chanted magic spells. Sprinkle them in the water and leave the place at once. I think the results will impress you."

"Thank you! Thank you!" Glaucus took the bag. "I will never forget you."

"No," Circe said. "You will never forget me."

Now every day Scylla liked to swim in a pool at Rhegium which lies near the steep rocks of Zancle. When the sun was at its hottest, she would dive into the crystal waters of the pool, then stretch herself out on the beach to dry. Glaucus found this out and one day, before she arrived, emptied the contents of the leather pouch on the surface. The roots that Circe had prepared were an ugly black, and as they struck the water they hissed angrily. But not for a minute did he believe that they would do anything but win his love over to him.

Scylla arrived a short time later. As usual, she plunged into the pool, unaware that it had been polluted. She swam slowly but steadily, enjoying the cool of the water beneath the heat of the sun. Then, still dripping, she lay down on the beach and fell asleep.

She was awoken by a low growling. She half-opened her eyes, then gasped in terror. A ferocious dog was sitting at her feet. There was another growl and she opened her eyes completely. Now she saw that there were no fewer than six of the monsters. She was surrounded by them. And these were no ordinary dogs. Their eyes bulged out of skulls that sat awkwardly on bony necks. Their skin was pitch black and hairless. Their teeth were shark-like.

Shuddering, terrified, she moved her arms an inch at a time, reaching for the sand behind her. If she could just pull herself clear without disturbing them . . . She hooked her hand into the sand and dragged herself backwards. As one, the six dogs followed her. Her heart was beating so painfully that she thought it would burst, but again she tried to ease herself away. She moved another six inches. The dogs moved another six inches. Then her nerve broke. She stood up and tried to run.

And then she realised with horror what had happened to her.

She could not run from the dogs. She could never run from the dogs. For the six animals were part of her, growing out of her. She was standing on twenty-four legs. The horrible heads were sprouting out of her waist. With a ghastly scream, she scuttled back from the edge of the sea, moving like some grotesque spider. But the dogs bayed with delight. And far away, on the island of Aeaea, Circe laughed too.

Scylla remained where she was and ever after sailors

went in fear of her, for she had no control over the six dogs which would tear travellers limb from limb and then slowly suck the pieces down.

And what of Glaucus?

"Leaves will grow in the sea and seaweed on the mountain tops before my feelings for Scylla change," he had said. But of course, leaves do grow in the sea and, as there are many underwater mountains, seaweed can be said to grow on mountain tops. Gradually his memory of Scylla and the rejection he had suffered faded. Then his old cheerfulness returned and he swam away to seek his fortune in the great expanse of the world's oceans.

But he never again went anywhere near the island of Aeaea.

# THE ACHILLES HEEL
## GREEK

This is the story of the greatest of all the Greek heroes. Achilles the fierce. Achilles the strong. Achilles the most courageous man who ever lived. It is also a story of that most terrible time in the history of Ancient Greece – about fourteen hundred years before the birth of Christ – when so many of its noblest princes were to fall in the nine long years of war at Troy.

You must imagine the city, vast and impregnable, its massive walls facing out towards a black, tormented sea. Overhead, the sky is thick with the smoke that pours out of the funeral pyres and from the forges where the blacksmiths work day and night, hammering at swords and shields, sharpening spears and arrowheads, fashioning the weapons of death. It is cold. A wind sweeps across the fields and a remorseless drizzle falls, stabbing at the pools that have formed in the mud, the water swirling round suddenly red as it mixes with the blood from the day's fighting. Between the city of the Trojans and the tents of the Greeks nothing moves. Both sides are sleeping.

This is the scene that was to shape the legend of the life of Achilles. This was where he was to meet his death.

### The Parents of Achilles

Achilles's mother was Thetis, a Nereid – one of the fifty nymphs of the sea who come to the aid of sailors – and an Immortal. His father was Peleus, King of the Myrmidons, but a mortal. The difference between the parents was to be the ruin of the marriage, for Thetis had been forced to marry Peleus against her own wishes. There had been a time when Zeus had loved Thetis but she had coldly rejected him. In revenge, Zeus had decreed that she should never marry an Immortal, a command that had infuriated the proud Thetis.

"How can I live with a mere mortal?" she had cried. "See what happens to mortal men with the passing of years. Their skin withers and their bellies sag. Their hair turns grey and their eyes become weak. No more can they run and fight. The passion within them grows cold. Am I to live with a decrepit, senile old man when I remain young and beautiful? Am I to see my children grow old and die when I remain alive? It is unjust! It is an outrage!"

The marriage went ahead, but when her first child was born she stole it away and, holding it by the heel, dipped it in the chill water of the River Styx which winds its way through the Underworld. In this way did she make her child immortal. But she made one mistake, a mistake that was one day to prove fatal. For she forgot to immerse the heel itself and that part of the baby remained mortal.

When Peleus found out what his wife had done, he was furious. A mortal himself, he had wanted his son to grow up the same way. He therefore snatched the baby away – before Thetis had even had time to breast-feed it. For this reason, because his lips had never touched his mother's breast, the baby was called Achilles which means "no lips".

## The Childhood of Achilles

Peleus and Thetis parted company immediately after this, Thetis returning to her home in the sea. Achilles was then entrusted to the care of Cheiron to be brought up amongst the olive trees on the slopes of Mount Pelion. Cheiron was a Centaur, half-man and half-horse – but unlike many of the Centaurs he was both gentle and wise.

Cheiron loved Achilles as though he were his own son. He fed the boy on the flesh of lions to give him courage and on sweet honeycombs to make him run swiftly. Who better was there to teach him how to ride and how to hunt? He also taught him the arts of pipe-playing and healing and the immortal Calliope, one of the nine Muses, visited the cave to teach him how to sing. Soon Achilles had grown into a youth of extraordinary beauty as well as great skill. His body was broad-shouldered and muscular. His hair tumbled down around his neck in a mass of golden curls. It is said that at the age of six he could outrun a full-grown stag and kill it with his own hands.

But while Achilles played in the sun on Mount Pelion, the clouds of war were gathering. It had been at the wedding of his own parents that Eris, goddess of discord, had sown the first seeds of disaster in the form of the golden apple that she had presented "to the fairest". Already Paris had made his choice and stolen Helen away as his prize. And throughout Greece, warriors and princes were coming together, forming the great army that would soon sail to Troy.

Now Thetis had been given a prophecy. The prophecy

stated simply that were Achilles to sail for Troy, he would never return. Although she had allowed Peleus to steal her child, she was still devoted to him and now she hurried to Mount Pelion in an attempt to save him from his fate that was as vain as it was desperate. Dressing him up as a woman, she took him to the court of Lycomedes, King of Scyros, hoping that he would be able to hide there, safe from the searching eyes of the Greek kings.

### Achilles Goes to War

While Achilles wasted his days amongst the women of Scyros, the main protagonists of the Trojan War were coming together and travelling the country in search of warriors prepared to fight – and die – with them.

There was Menelaus, king of Sparta and the leader of the Greek forces. For Helen had been his wife and it had been his honour that had been assailed when Paris had stolen her. With him was Agamemnon, king of Mycenae, his brother. Nobody would fight more valiantly in the Trojan War. Nobody would die more treacherously after it. And there was Odysseus, who had himself feigned madness to try to avoid going to Troy and who would be condemned to wander for ten years before he saw his home again.

It was Odysseus who came to Scyros in search of Achilles, for a soothsayer had warned that Troy could not be taken without him. Faced with the bland smiles of the king and a palace that was filled – on the face of it – only with women, Odysseus was forced to resort to a trick. First he presented the women with a great heap of gifts: jewels, perfumes and beautiful dresses, but also one sword and one shield. Then, while they argued over who got what, he gave the signal for his soldiers outside the palace to sound their trumpets and shout as if an army had just attacked. At once, one of the "women" threw off her wig and seized the shield and sword and in this way was Achilles discovered and recruited to the army.

And so Achilles set out for Troy, taking with him a magic spear that only he could wield – a gift from Cheiron – and also a chest inlaid with ivory and jewels and packed with blankets, tunics and cloaks to protect him against the wind – a present from his grieving mother. He was accompanied by his cousin, Patroclus, who was older than him but neither as skilful nor as well-born. Achilles loved him more than anyone else in the world.

### Achilles at Troy

Achilles was the second Greek to leap onto the Trojan coast. He would have been the first had Thetis not warned him that the first to land would also be the first to die. This honour, if so it can be called, was taken by one Protesilaus who was promptly run through by Hector, the prince of Troy.

The first battle was fought on the beach and Achilles, leading his father's faithful Myrmidons, soon proved that he deserved his reputation for valour. In the heat of the fighting, he found himself confronted by Cycnus, the son of Poseidon and a ferocious warrior. In the first twenty minutes of the battle he had killed no fewer than a hundred Greeks and their blood coated every inch of his armour, and dripped out of his hair.

Achilles threw himself at him and the two fought furiously. Cycnus was more like a beast than a man, snarling in anger, his eyes wide with blood-lust. And he was seemingly invincible. Achilles would slash at him with his sword but either his opponent moved faster than the eye could see or the blade passed straight through him without so much as breaking his skin. He thrust his spear at him, but Cycnus caught the point in his bare hands and, with a horrible laugh, turned it aside.

At last Achilles managed to force him back, using the hilt of his sword to bludgeon him on the side of the head. Cycnus staggered and tripped over. At once, Achilles was on top of him, straddling him with his legs. Cycnus screamed in anger. Achilles tore off his helmet and forced the strap round the Trojan's neck, squeezing with all his strength. While the Greek army forced the Trojans back off the beach to win their first victory, Cycnus groaned and breathed his last.

In the weeks that followed, Achilles added victory to victory, death to death until his name was the most feared in the entire Greek army. Priam, the king of Troy, lost no less than three of his sons to Achilles, his beloved Troilus chased into the temple of Apollo and speared on the very altar itself. With the Myrmidons behind him, Achilles ravaged the countryside, seizing the Trojan herds of cattle and sacking the city of Lyrnessus. It was here that he discovered the beautiful princess Briseis. Her father had died in the fighting and Achilles, who had fallen in love with her, took her back to his tent to be his serving-maid.

## The Wrath of Achilles

It was at this time (in the spring) that Achilles had his second argument with King Agamemnon. They had almost come to blows once when Achilles had suggested that the king of Mycenae had only entered the war out of a sense of guilt and didn't really want to fight at all. Agamemnon had retorted by reminding Achilles of the time he had spent disguised as a girl and after that the two had never been friends.

This new, more serious, argument concerned Briseis. Agamemnon had found himself an equally beautiful captive but had been forced to send her back to Troy when it was discovered that she was a priestess. So now the king seized Briseis for himself, which angered Achilles so much that he stormed off into his tent, refusing to have anything more to do with the war.

At first nobody believed that so great a warrior could behave in such a way, but as the days passed and Achilles failed to appear, they realised he meant just what he said. The Trojans, when their spies reported the news, returned to the battlefield with renewed vigour. This was virtually their first piece of good fortune since the Greeks had landed.

The morale of an army can win a war, and suddenly it seemed that the Trojans had gained the upper hand. A daring sortie was led by Hector, the eldest son of King

Priam, and the Greek lines were broken. Both Agamemnon and Odysseus were wounded in the fighting and while the Greeks scattered in panic, Hector pressed on towards their fleet. If he were able to burn their ships and cut the supply lines, he might well end the whole enterprise – but still Achilles refused to fight.

It was Patroclus who saved the day. The flames were already devouring the first ship, black smoke curling up the masts and brilliant sparks cascading onto the water, when Patroclus ran forward, wearing the armour of Achilles, and hurled his spear into the mass of Trojans. He would have been cut down where he stood but for the fact that he so resembled Achilles that the Trojans mistook him for his cousin and fled. Then, while Greek soldiers put out the fire, Patroclus regrouped the rest of the army and chased the fleeing Trojans towards the walls of the city.

Patroclus had lived his whole life in the shadow of Achilles. Where his cousin had been exalted, he had been ignored. Where his cousin was famous, he was unknown. Now, for the first and last time, he found himself the undisputed leader of the suddenly fearless Greek forces and a hero in his own right. He chased the Trojans right back to the walls, while Achilles, hearing what was happening, hastily assembled his Myrmidons. But Patroclus relied on luck as much as skill and now his luck ran out. A chance blow caught him between the shoulder blades. His helmet was torn off and at the same moment his spear splintered. Blinded, he staggered away from the wall of Troy, then screamed and twisted round as a sword was driven into his chest. Dying, he tried to lift himself out of the mud. That was how Hector found him. One blow and it was over.

When Achilles came upon the body of his cousin, the Greek soldiers were fighting furiously to protect it. With a cry of anger and grief he threw himself into the battle, striking out left and right, forming a bloody circle around the corpse. At last, as the sun was setting, the Trojans retired and Achilles was able to pick up the body of Patroclus and carry it back to the Greek ships that he had saved.

He was buried with full honours beside the sea, the dying sun casting a scarlet banner across the water. Agamemnon, though wounded, came from his tent, bringing Briseis, to make his peace with Achilles. And Achilles, standing beside his cousin's grave, swore revenge on the man who had killed him.

### Achilles and Hector

If Achilles was the pride of the Greek army, then Hector was his equivalent in the Trojan. The two men were natural opponents. They were even physical opposites, with Hector's jet-black hair and dark skin. Moreover, although the two had yet to encounter one another on the field, a deep hatred existed between them and each sought revenge on the other, Achilles for the death of Patroclus, Hector for the loss of three brothers, Troilus and Mestor killed and Lycaon captured and sold into slavery for the price of a silver bowl.

Hector had challenged Achilles to single combat once, but that had been at the time when he was refusing to fight.

Now he accepted and for one day the war was suspended, both sides standing back to watch the confrontation.

It was a brilliant morning. The waves, hurrying towards the field of combat, seemed to throw precious stones onto the sand as they crashed against the shore. A soft breeze brushed across the Greek camp, tussling the hair of the waiting soldiers. There was a murmur as the gates of Troy swung open and a single figure stepped out, dressed in black and silver armour, a sword in one hand, a spear in the other. Then the flaps of Achilles's tent were pulled back and the murmur became a gasp. Thetis had visited her son that night, bringing with her new armour forged by the immortal Hephaestus himself. Now, as Achilles stood in the sunlight, he seemed to be carved out of solid gold and the reflection of the sun around him was almost blinding.

Perhaps Hector knew at that moment that he was doomed. Achilles was relentless, unstoppable. Saying nothing, he approached the Trojan, his feet pounding in the dust. As soon as he was within range, Hector hurled his spear. Achilles raised his shield and the spear clattered uselessly to one side. Then Hector ran, not because he was afraid but because he hoped to tire his enemy. Three times he circled the walls of Troy but when he stopped and looked round, Achilles was still the same distance from him, barely out of breath.

Then, with the shouts of the Trojan forces above them and the Greek forces all around them, the two men joined in combat. So ferociously did they fight that when sword struck sword the spark could be seen a mile away. Hector was perhaps the stronger. But Achilles was the faster and, watching from the walls, the Trojans let out a great cry when he dodged one blow, carried his sword in low and ran their prince through the heart.

Hector crumpled to his knees.

"Achilles!" he whispered, the blood curtaining over his lip. "Let my parents have my body. Let me be buried honourably."

"Never!" Achilles cried. He twisted his sword and watched the light in Hector's eyes go out.

Then he took the body and, while King Priam looked on, helpless and in horror, he fastened it by the feet to his chariot and rode off around the city. Three more times he circled Troy, dragging Hector behind him. At last he rode back to his camp, taking the body with him. But the ordeal was not yet over for the Trojans. Although they offered their prince's weight in gold for the return of the corpse, Achilles refused. And every day at dawn he would taunt them with it, whipping up his horses around the walls, dragging his enemy in a cloud of dust behind him.

Every day for a week Achilles did the same, deaf to the lamentations of the Trojans and even to the pleas of his own mother. Such was his grief at the loss of Patroclus. At last, the gates of Troy opened and King Priam himself rode out, accompanied only by one young soldier and by four servants carrying a litter. Under the flag of truce, he proceeded to the tent of Achilles and there threw himself onto the ground.

"Achilles!" the old man wept. "You have proved yourself

a great warrior, but have you the compassion to prove yourself a great man? You have killed my eldest child, the son I most loved and in whom I had the most pride. What times are these that fine soldiers and princes must perish in the bloom of their youth! Now, I beg you, show pity to an old man. See – I bring you Hector's weight in gold. Will you not be moved by a father's tears? Think on your own father and let me lay the remains of Troy's noblest prince to rest. Let me bury my son."

Then Achilles wept too – for his cousin Patroclus, for the futility of war and for the man he had almost become himself. He gave orders for the body of Hector to be carried back to Troy and called for a truce of twelve days in which the funeral solemnities could be prepared.

### The Death of Achilles

The war dragged on. Amongst those who died were, on the Trojan side, Penthesileia, queen of the Amazons and one of the few heroines of mythology, and Memnon, the Ethiopian leader whose skin was as black as ebony and who was said to be the handsomest man alive. The Greeks had their losses too. Antilochus, young, swift and courageous, died at the hand of Memnon and Thersites, the ugliest soldier at Troy, was actually slain by Achilles himself as the result of an argument.

But for Achilles too, time was drawing in.

After the death of Hector, he had fought as bravely as ever, the differences between him and Agamemnon forgotten. On many occasions he routed the Trojans, often coming close to breaching the walls of the city itself. But he had made himself the target of too many enemies, and not all of them were human ones. Poseidon, the sea-god, still demanded vengeance for the death of his son Cycnus, while Apollo had been enraged by the killing of Troilus, which had taken place in his own temple.

So one day in the thick of the fighting, Poseidon whispered to Paris – the man who, more than any other, had begun the war – that Achilles was not invulnerable, while Apollo guided his hand. For the gods remembered how Thetis had held him when she dipped him in the Styx, and now Paris let loose a poisoned arrow which struck him in the heel.

At once Achilles fainted and had to be carried off the field by his Myrmidons. Doctors were called but already the poison had spread through his blood and that night, with Thetis beside him and the stars blazing silver in the sky, he died.

The Greek army mourned for seventeen days and seventeen nights and the nine Muses themselves came down into the world to sing his dirge. On the eighteenth day his body was burnt on a great pyre beside the sea.

And as the smoke rose over the crashing waves, the two armies clashed once again in a war which was tainted by grey despair, a war which was suddenly less glorious and less heroic than it had once seemed.

# THE MARES OF DIOMEDES
## GREEK

Hercules, son of Zeus and the mortal Alcmene, was the strongest man who ever lived. It was said that at close range, his biceps looked like the Alps and that he could put a man in hospital for six weeks just by shaking hands. You would certainly have been ill-advised to kick sand in the face of Hercules had you seen him at the beach. Not unless you wanted to find yourself several feet under the sand with your legs tied in a knot behind your head.

When Hercules was only a tiny baby, the goddess Hera (ever jealous of her husband's infidelities) sent two enormous snakes to destroy him. Now each snake was several times larger than Hercules, with bulging eyes, ferocious teeth and a spitting, poisonous tongue. But Hercules simply took one in each hand, giggled, and squeezed. And by the time his nurse arrived to see what all the hissing, spitting, giggling and gurgling was about, the baby was sound asleep with two very surprised snakes lying dead at the bottom of his crib.

Hera, who never forgot a slight no matter how slight it might be, remained his immortal enemy for life and later on succeeded in driving him mad. In his madness, Hercules thought he saw six of his worst enemies and immediately killed them all, only to find that they weren't enemies at all but his own children. For this unfortunate crime, the Oracle at Delphi sent him to Argolis, to work for twelve years under the orders of King Eurystheus. And that is how the famous Twelve Labours of Hercules came about.

Hercules was not at all happy about having to work for a man who, if placed in a boxing ring with him, would have lasted approximately 0.5 of a second. But he could not disobey the Oracle. He was at least well equipped for the labours that would follow. His father, Zeus, gave him an unbreakable shield. The sea-god, Poseidon, gave him a troop of horses. Apollo, god of the sun, gave him a bow and arrows trimmed with eagle feathers. From the messenger-god, Hermes, he received a sword; from Athene, goddess of wisdom, a robe; and from the lame god Hephaestus, a breastplate made of gold. In the next few months, he would need them all.

His first challenge was the Nemean Lion, a gigantic, seemingly invincible beast that managed to bite off one of his fingers before he throttled it. Next came the Lernaean Hydra. This was the famous monster with nine heads that grew two more heads every time one was cut off. In the end, Hercules set fire to the whole lot at once, so destroying it – although he lost part of one toe in the struggle.

Not all the labours involved killing things. The fifth task, for example, was to clean the stables of King Augeias and this could have been the most difficult of all. For the stables were filthy. No fewer than three thousand oxen were kept in them and nobody had been near the place with a mop or a bucket and spade for thirty years. You could smell the Augeian stables from the far side of the Peloponnese and the fields surrounding them for five miles in every direction were not green but brown. As it turned out, much to the annoyance of King Eurystheus, Hercules didn't even get his hands dirty. He simply diverted two rivers into the stables and the rushing waters did all the work for him.

It must be said that King Eurystheus did not particularly like Hercules. The king was a thin, flabby man who got hay fever in the summer and influenza in the winter. Hercules was massive, in perfect health, the son of a god. And Hercules could crush bricks to powder in his bare hands. King Eurystheus couldn't even grow a decent beard. So the king hoped that Hercules would either fail in one of his labours or, better still, die trying. And with the mares of Diomedes, he thought he had found a task that would rid the world of the hero once and for all.

"I congratulate you, Hercules," he said. "So far you have managed to clean the Augeian stables. You have killed the Nemean Lion, the Lernaean Hydra and the Stymphalian Birds. And you have captured the Cretan Bull, the Ceryneian Hind and the . . . er . . . wild boar of Erymanthus." He smiled nervously, trying not to remember the wild boar which had frightened him so much at the time that he had dived head-first into a bronze jar and stayed there all afternoon. "Seven labours well done. Well done indeed!

"I thought for labour number eight, I would give you something a little easier. No monsters this time! No. All I want are the four mares of the Thracian king Diomedes. I'm afraid he's rather attached to them. I understand that he even keeps them in stables made of solid bronze. So I dare say he won't be too happy when you steal them. Still, that should be no problem for a man like you. Or should I say a demi-god? I mean, you never get hay fever or influenza, do you? You can do anything!"

And with a little chuckle that concealed an unpleasant secret, King Eurystheus climbed down from the throne and went for another – useless – work-out in the palace gymnasium.

Hercules set off at once, travelling with a servant called Abderus. Together, the two men arrived in the Thracian town of Tirida where the four mares of Diomedes were said to be stabled. All they had to do was to find out where – and this proved no problem as the bronze stables, glinting in the sunlight, could be seen for miles around. What did prove to be a problem, though, were the Bistones.

The Bistones were the soldiers of King Diomedes and a more violent, more bloodthirsty mob would be impossible to imagine. Wherever they went, they were armed to the teeth. In fact even their teeth were armed . . . specially sharpened so that if by chance they lost all the rest of their weapons, they could still bite people. They carried two swords, a shield, a bow and arrows, an axe, a ball on a chain, a sling and as many knives as they could find room for. Night and day they wore heavy armour and chain mail shirts. They feared nothing – except rust. Fortunately, however, it didn't rain very often in Thrace and never during important battles. A Bistone was only really happy when he was hacking someone to pieces. Even being hacked to pieces was all right as far as a Bistone was concerned. That was how violent they were.

Anyway, Hercules and Abderus were surprised to find only two Bistones guarding the precious mares of King Diomedes and these were easily dealt with. Hercules crept up on them and broke their necks while Abderus unchained the horses. Again, both of them were a little puzzled to find such elegant animals secured with such heavy, iron chains – but as everything seemed to be going well, they thought no more of it.

And the mares of Diomedes were elegant; there could be no doubt of that. Pure white, they were as perfectly formed as statues, with bright blue eyes and wonderfully untamed manes. They showed no fear as Abderus released them but seemed to lean towards him, nuzzling his collar as he led them out of the stables.

They followed the two men obediently as they left the town of Tirida and made their way towards the coast, where the ship was waiting to take them back to Argolis. The only time they showed any fear was when the silence of the late afternoon was shattered by a great cry of outrage. The mares trembled, Abderus went white and even Hercules scratched his head. For the two dead guards and the theft of the horses had been discovered. And right now ten thousand extremely angry Bistones were charging out of the town and up the hillside towards them.

"Abderus! Take the horses!" Hercules commanded.

"Lead them over the brow of the hill and wait for me on the other side."

"What are you going to do, master?" Abderus cried.

"Don't worry! I've got a plan."

"But there are ten thousand of them!"

"Ten thousand?" Hercules shrugged his shoulders and smiled. "No problem."

But even the strength of Hercules might have proved useless against the twenty thousand swords, ten thousand shields . . . and so on of the Bistones, had he not noticed a peculiarity in the landscape on his way to Tirida. The town lay in a deep valley near the coast. The edge of the sea was actually above the town and moreover, there was a single, huge rock lying at the top of the hill between the two of them. All he had to do was to move the stone and the sea would rush along the newly formed channel and down into the valley.

As soon as Abderus and the mares had reached the safety of the shore, he set to work. The stone was vast, ten times his own height and several hundred times his weight. Setting his back against it, he could have been leaning against a small mountain, but he seemed unaware of the challenge. Closing his eyes and gritting his teeth, the water lapping at his feet, he pushed.

The rock tottered but refused to roll. The Bistones were half-way up the side of the valley now. Already they were shooting off their arrows, the ones at the back accidentally killing the ones at the front in their over-enthusiasm. He pushed again, harder this time. The rock swayed on its base, but still clung to the earth as if glued there. The first Bistone had reached the top of the hill and had drawn both of his swords. Hercules gave a great cry and pushed a third time. Like a loose tooth, the rock finally came free, and as Hercules threw himself out of the way, the waters rushed to fill the hole.

Fifty of the Bistones were crushed by the massive stone as it spun down the hill. Another fifty were killed by their friends as they tried to get out of its way. The rest of them were drowned. The sea exploded through the gap in the hillside, a thousand white horses racing to replace the four that had been stolen. Nothing could stand in its way. Trees were torn out of the ground, houses smashed into a whirling mass of brick and broken wood. In seconds the entire town of Tirida had disappeared underneath a spreading lake, a lake on whose dirty water floated the army of Bistones, swirling round like dead flies.

Meanwhile, on the other side of the hill beside the sea, Abderus was waiting with the horses, quite unaware of what was going on. He was also unaware of something else. For what King Eurystheus had neglected to mention was that the mares of Diomedes were not quite as elegant as they seemed. In fact they were nothing short of monsters, feeding not on hay or on sugar but on the raw flesh of human beings. It had often been a joke of King Diomedes to feed his unsuspecting guests to them. Unfortunately for Abderus, there had not been a guest at the palace for a week.

"Hey – girls – you look hungry," the servant muttered as he waited for Hercules to deal with the ten thousand Bistones. It was certainly true that the mares were looking at him with hunger sharp in their eyes. "Would you like some grass then?" The servant smiled foolishly. "Who wants some grass then?"

He picked up a clump and held it out to the horses.

"Who wants some lovely . . ."

The first of the horses opened its mouth. Its teeth were yellow, and now its eyes burnt red.

". . . graaaaagh!"

By the time Hercules returned, there was nothing left of Abderus apart from a few bones, and a little blood flecking the white mouths of the mares. And the four horses were just a little fatter than they had been when he left them. Carefully, he took hold of their chains, understanding now why they needed them. And not once, on the long voyage home, did his eyes leave them.

King Eurystheus was in the bath when he got back to Argolis. The king was in a good mood and had been for some time.

"I expect we'll be hearing about Hercules any day now," he was saying to the slave who was washing his back. "I can hardly wait. He'll have beaten the Bistones and stolen the mares – but he'll have never guessed just *what* he's stolen. Not, that is, until they eat him! Oh dear me, yes! That'll teach Mister Muscles."

The words were no sooner out of his mouth than

there was a strange sound from the room next door – a sort of clatter.

"What the . . .?" he began.

And then the four mares of Diomedes trotted merrily into the bathroom, their hooves striking against the mosaic floor. Eurystheus screamed, swallowed a mouthful of bath water and screamed again.

"Your horses, sire," Hercules said, walking in behind them.

King Eurystheus had run three-and-a-half miles before he realized he was still completely naked. And it would be months before he would sleep again without nightmares. The nightmares of Diomedes.

# PANDORA'S BOX
## GREEK

There are some who say that the original creator of mankind was Prometheus, that he fashioned the first man in the image of the gods using clay and water taken from Panopeus in Phocis. Prometheus was a Titan, one of the race of giants who fought an unsuccessful war against Zeus and the other gods – and it is certainly true that he was a great deal wiser than his brothers.

For he alone knew that the war was doomed to failure. He realized that, huge and immensely strong though the Titans undoubtedly were, they also suffered from a common trait amongst giants. They just weren't very bright. A Titan might tear up a mountain instead of going round it, but he would probably find out later on that he was going the wrong way anyway. A Titan might be able to hurl a rock the size of Gibraltar a hundred miles or more, but he would invariably miss whatever he was aiming for.

On the other hand, of course, the gods were as quick-witted as they were skilled in the art of war. First there was Zeus, the king of Olympus, armed with his devastating thunderbolts.

Then there was Poseidon with his trident, Apollo with his golden arrows, the invisible Hermes . . . it was an invincible army, and Prometheus could see that his brothers would be lost against it.

Lose was what they did. Most of them were sent to a

dark and damp prison in the depths of Tartarus. Atlas — perhaps the most famous Titan of all — was condemned to hold up the heavens on his shoulders for all time. But Prometheus, who had let everyone know that he was neutral from the start, got away scot free. That was when he created man.

Prometheus loved men in the same way people love their pets. He was immensely proud of everything they did, boasted about them to almost anyone who would listen, and generally fussed over them in every way possible. Instead of feeding them with food, however, he fed them knowledge — scraps of information that he picked up from Athene, the goddess of wisdom and his only real friend in Olympus. One day she would tell him about mathematics and straight away he would rush down to earth to pass it on. The next day it might be art or architecture, the day after that science or engineering. It's strange to think that our entire civilization could have been handed down to us rather in the manner of dog biscuits, but that is how it was.

As the years passed and mankind became more intelligent, Zeus, who had been watching all this from his celestial throne, grew uneasy.

"I am a little worried about these human beings," he remarked to his wife, Hera, one day over a goblet of wine.

"What about them?" Hera asked.

"Well . . . I just wonder if they're not getting a bit . . . above themselves. Where will it all lead to? That's what I want to know. Today the rudiments of geometry, tomorrow it could be genetic surgery."

"So what are you going to do about it?"

"I don't know. But I'm keeping my eye on them!"

Zeus might have been a jealous god, but he was not cruel enough to destroy the newly formed human race. And so mankind continued to flourish. Things came to a head, however, one day in a place called Sicyon. The trouble was caused by a question of ownership.

Prometheus had taught man to stay on the right side of the gods by regularly sacrificing the best animals from their herds. A special sacrificial bull had been chosen for Zeus at Sicyon, but the question was, which part should be reserved for the god and which parts should the men (who had worked hard to raise the animal in the first place) be allowed to keep? As usual, Prometheus acted as the mediator in the dispute but, unwisely, he decided to play a trick on Zeus.

When the bull had been killed and cut up, he took two sacks. Into one of these, he put all the most succulent portions of meat – the rump and the fillet, the sirloin and the rib – but concealed them beneath the stomach-bag which was all white and rubbery and generally disgusting to look at. Into the other went the bones and the gristle, the eyeballs and the hooves . . . in short, all the most unappetizing parts of the bull. But these were covered with a layer of fat to make them look as delicious as possible.

Then Prometheus took both sacks and knelt before Zeus.

"Oh, mighty king!" he said. "Why should there be any

quarrel between you and the little pink creatures who inhabit the world below? Take this matter of sacrifice. It seems that nobody can decide who should get exactly what. Well, as you are the king of Olympus, why don't you choose for yourself? I have divided the bull between these two sacks. Which one do you want?"

Zeus, who had never suspected that a Titan could think up such a scheme, was completely deceived. He chose the bones and the fat and ever since that time the gods have received nothing else from the sacrifice. When he found out how Prometheus had tricked him, however, he was furious.

"Man may have his steak," he thundered. "But he will eat it raw!"

And with those words, he reached out with one hand and snatched all the fire from the world.

It seemed that mankind had got the worst deal after all. Without fire they could take no pleasure in their food and once the sun had gone down, they could only stay indoors, huddled under animal skins for warmth. But Prometheus was willing to do anything to help his creation and one day, while Zeus was out having one of his many affairs, he stole up to Olympus. For he still had one friend in the home of the gods: Athene. Hearing him knocking on a side-door, the goddess of wisdom unbolted it and let him in. Then Prometheus rode up to the sun and, using his bare hands, broke off a blazing fire-brand. This he carried back to earth, thrusting it into a giant fennel-leaf. And in this way people were once again able to enjoy their meat *grillé*.

But this time Prometheus had gone too far. When Zeus heard how he had been defied for a second time, his anger knew no bounds.

"Prometheus!" he cried. "You crossed me once and I forgave you because of your loyalty to me in the war of the Titans. But this time there can be no forgiveness. This time you must pay for your crime."

And so saying, he seized Prometheus and chained him to a pillar on the freezing slopes of the Caucasus Mountains. But if this was not punishment enough, worse was to come. Every morning a huge vulture landed on the wretched Titan's chest and even as he screamed in rage and horror, tore out his liver and devoured it. And every night, while Prometheus shivered in the sub-zero temperatures, his liver grew whole again. In this way the horrible torture could be repeated again and again until the end of time.

Zeus punished mankind too. But as man had only offended indirectly, his punishment was of another sort.

First he visited the crippled god Hephaestus who worked at a great forge in Olympus with twenty bellows pumping twenty-four hours a day. Although ugly and misshapen himself, no blacksmith was more skilled than Hephaestus.

"I want you to make me a woman," the king of the gods commanded. "I want her to be more beautiful than any woman ever seen on the face of the earth. She must be perfect. As perfect as a goddess."

Hephaestus did as he was told. He had only ever

disobeyed Zeus once. That had been just before he became the crippled god. Now he fashioned a woman out of clay, moulding her perfect features with his own hands. He commissioned the four winds to breathe life into her and asked all the goddesses to help dress her in their finest clothes and jewels.

The result was Pandora.

When Zeus saw the blacksmith-god's work, he was well pleased and instructed Hermes to carry her into the world at once. There she was married to a certain King Epimetheus, the brother of Prometheus and the only other Titan who had not joined in the war against the gods.

Now Epimetheus had been warned never to trust the gifts of Zeus, but seeing the terrible fate that had befallen his brother, he was too afraid to refuse. Moreover, he had to admit that Pandora was beautiful. You'd have had to be mad to think otherwise. When she walked into the room, men fell silent and all eyes turned on her. Whatever she said, people would agree. When she made jokes, the laughter would continue for several minutes. Whatever she did was greeted with applause. And Epimetheus did feel rather proud to be married to her.

Unfortunately, the things Pandora said were never really worth listening to, for she was not a very intelligent creature. Her jokes were in truth extremely unfunny. She did very little because she was impossibly lazy and if Epimetheus was glad to be her husband, she made him a poor and unfaithful wife. For this was the revenge of Zeus.

He had made her as shallow and as coquettish as she was beautiful. And she was to cause more trouble to mankind than any woman before or any woman since.

For Epimetheus owned a large, ebony box which was kept in a special room in his palace, guarded day and night. In this box he had collected and imprisoned all the things that could harm mankind. It was the one room in the palace that Pandora was forbidden to enter and naturally it was the one room that most aroused her curiosity.

"I bet you keep all sorts of super things in that big, black box of yours," she would say in her syrupy voice. "Why don't you let your little Pandy look inside?"

"It is not for you, my dear," Epimetheus would reply. "You should leave well alone."

"But . . ."

"No, no, my love. No one may open the box."

"Then you don't love me," Pandora would say, crossing her arms and pouting. "And I'm not going to love you any more – not ever!"

They had this conversation many times until the day when Pandora couldn't resist her curiosity any longer. For despite everything Epimetheus had told her about the box, she still believed that it contained some special treat that he was holding back from her.

"I'll show him . . . the old bossy-boots," she muttered to herself.

Waiting until Epimetheus was out, she managed to talk her way past the guards and into the room. She had stolen the key from beside his bed and nobody thought to stop her. Was she not, after all, the king's wife and the mistress of the house? Her whole body trembling, she knelt down beside the box. It was smaller and older than she had expected. It was also a little surprising (not to say upsetting) that the padlock which fastened it should be in the shape of a human skull. But she was certain it would contain treasure such as would make all her own diamonds and pearls seem like mere pebbles, treasure that would make her the envy of the world. She turned the key and opened the box . . .

. . . and at once all the spites and problems that Epimetheus had for so long kept locked up, exploded into the world. Old age, hard work, sickness . . . they flew out in a great cloud of buzzing, stinging, biting insects. It was as if Pandora had accidentally split the atom. One moment she was standing there with a foolish grin on her face. The next she was screaming in the heart of an intense darkness that had, in seconds, stripped her of her beauty and brought her out in a thousand boils.

At that moment, all the things that make life difficult today streamed out of Pandora's box and into the world:

Old age, hard work, sickness, vice, anger, envy, lust, covetousness, spite, sarcasm, cynicism, violence, intolerance, injustice, infidelity, famine, drought, pestilence, war, religious persecution, apartheid, taxation, inflation, pollution, unemployment, fascism, racism, sexism, terrorism, communism, nepotism, patriotism, nihilism, totalitarianism, plagiarism, vandalism, tourism, paranoia, schizophrenia, kleptomania, claustrophobia, xenophobia, hypochondria, insomnia, megalomania, narrow-mindedness, thoughtlessness, selfishness, bribery, corruption, censorship, gluttony, pornography, delinquency, vulgarity, bureaucracy, complacency, obesity, acne, diplomatic immunity, traffic congestion, party political broadcasts, fast food, urban development, modern architecture, muzak, organized crime, dolphinariums, advertising, alcoholism, drug addiction, monosodium glutamate, nicotine, nuclear waste, data processing, fanaticism, insanity, drizzle, elephant's-feet-wastepaper-baskets and much, much more.

At the last moment, Epimetheus managed to slam down the lid, by which time only one thing was left in the box: hope.

Which is just as well. For with all the problems that Pandora had released into the world, where would we be without it?

# THE GORGON'S HEAD
## GREEK

There was once a king called Polydectes who ruled on an island called Seriphos, and he fell in love with a woman who happened to live in his palace. This woman was called Danae and she had been found washed up on the shores of the island along with a young son called Perseus who now served Polydectes as a soldier.

Now although Polydectes loved Danae – who was still very beautiful – Danae did not feel quite the same way about Polydectes. For the king was really rather fat, he was inclined to be occasionally tyrannical and worst of all he had very bad breath. It was said that the king's breath could stop a Cyclops at ten paces – and don't forget that for a Cyclops ten paces is a very long way indeed.

Left to himself, Polydectes would have forced Danae to marry him, but of course there was Perseus to consider. The boy was strong, afraid of nothing and very quick-tempered . . . in short, just the sort to let fly with a sword if anyone laid a finger on his mother. Worse still, he was very popular on the island, and there would have been an uproar if something horrible had "accidentally" happened to him.

Well, the king thought about it for a time and at last he came up with a plan. He announced his marriage, but pretended that he was going to marry a girl called Hippodameia, the daughter of a friend of his. He then threw a great banquet and invited everyone in the neighbourhood.

Of course, everybody brought gifts. And of course, the gifts (like so many wedding presents) were completely useless. He got no less than seven wine-jugs, for example, and he already had more wine-jugs than he knew what to do with.

Nonetheless, there was no mistaking the value of the presents, which were all made of gold or silver or onyx or the finest marble. Nor could there be any mistaking the fact that when Perseus turned up at the banquet (he had also been invited), he arrived empty-handed. For Perseus, besides being very young, bold and strong, was also very poor.

When he saw Perseus, King Polydectes pretended to be furious. But secretly he was pleased, for he had known all along that Perseus wouldn't be able to afford a present.

"What, no wedding present!" he shouted.

There were gasps of surprise around the banqueting tables.

"Don't you know that it is a tradition to bring your sovereign a present when he decides to get married?"

"I don't have any money, sire," Perseus explained.

"No money! That's what comes of being a lazy good-for-nothing and a mummy's boy."

All these words were intended to make Perseus lose his temper, and they worked. For he went very red in the face and cried out:

"I am none of these things, sire. And to prove it, you can have anything you want for your wedding present. You only have to name it."

"Anything?" Polydectes asked, raising an eyebrow.

"Anything," Perseus said.

"Anything?" Polydectes insisted, raising the other eyebrow.

"Anything in the world," said Perseus.

"Then what I would like for my wedding present is a Gorgon's head. If you're so clever, bring me the head of a Gorgon."

Several of the courtiers, seated at the tables in the banqueting hall, fainted with sheer terror. The rest all lost their appetites.

"Very well, sire," Perseus said. "If the head of a Gorgon is what you want, the head of a Gorgon is what you shall have."

And with that, he stormed out of the room.

### The Three Gorgons

Of all the monsters, beasts, giants, dragons and creepy-crawlies in Ancient Greece, the Gorgons were perhaps the most gruesome. Men were petrified by them – literally.

There were three Gorgons. Sthenno and Euryale were immortal. The third and most fearsome, Medusa, was not – so she was the only one that Perseus had any chance of being able to kill.

The Gorgons had once been three very attractive young girls. Then Medusa had fallen in love with Poseidon, the god of the sea, and had slept with him in the temple of Athene, the goddess of wisdom. This had been most unwise. To punish Medusa for behaving improperly in her temple, Athene turned her – and her sisters with her – into the Gorgons. And that was how they became so ugly. Instead of teeth they had sharp tusks like wild boars. Their hands were made of bronze and they had golden wings on their shoulders. But what was most remarkable about these horrors was their hair. Their hair was made of living snakes, slimy green and silver snakes with hissing tongues and gleaming eyes. There were dozens of them, sprouting out of the Gorgons' skulls, writhing over their foreheads, curling round their necks and twisting over their shoulders. If you had ever had the misfortune to set eyes on a Gorgon ... you would have done absolutely nothing. For this was the cruellest part of King Polydectes's trick. Everyone who saw the face of a Gorgon became so frightened that they instantly turned to stone. The king knew Perseus would never get near them. Even if he found them he couldn't look at them. One look and he would be doomed.

Anyway, as soon as Perseus had set off on his seemingly hopeless mission, the coast was clear for Polydectes who immediately threw himself on Danae.

## The Goddess of Wisdom

Perseus had travelled far and searched for a long time but he had found no trace of either Medusa or her ugly sisters. One night he found himself sitting under a tree on the edge of a swamp in an unknown country. He was cold and he was alone. For the first time he wondered if he hadn't been a bit hasty in agreeing to the king's request.

It was at that moment that a figure suddenly appeared, stepping out of the flames of his bonfire. It was a woman, tall and beautiful and with bright eyes. On her head she wore a helmet. She carried a spear and a gleaming shield. Perseus recognized her at once because he had been taught about the gods and goddesses and besides (although he didn't know it at the time) she was in fact his aunt. The woman was Athene.

"Perseus," she said, standing before him. "I've come to help you because, although you were perhaps a bit silly to let King Polydectes trick you the way he did, I can see that you have a good heart and all the trimmings that usually make up a hero."

"Thank you, Athene," Perseus said. "I'm looking for . . . "

"I know who you're looking for," Athene snapped. "I'm not the goddess of wisdom for nothing, you know! But the only way to find the Gorgons is to ask their sisters the Grey Ones – who, by a happy coincidence, live in the swamp a few minutes from here. And you'll also have to know how to kill Medusa because (Polydectes didn't tell you this, the rotter!), anyone who sees her turns to stone."

"You mean . . . I can't even look at her?"

"Not directly. But I can tell you what to do."

"It's very kind of you, Athene," Perseus said.

"Don't mention it. As a matter of fact, I've never cared much for Medusa and it's about time someone got her. Now listen carefully, Perseus. Your life will depend on it . . . "

## The Grey Ones

A short while later, Perseus crept up on the Grey Ones who were sitting beside a bog arguing. They were always arguing.

The Grey Ones weren't exactly monsters but they were certainly most peculiar. They had been born with grey hair (which is how they got their name), and they had only one eye and one tooth between the three of them. They were called Enyo, Pemphredo and Deino.

As Perseus approached, this is what he heard.

"Can I have the tooth, please, Enyo?" Pemphredo was saying.

"Why?" Enyo asked.

"Because I want to eat an apple."

"But I'm eating a toffee."

"You can suck the toffee. I want the tooth!"

"All right. All right. Here it is, then."

"I can't see it."

"Haven't you got the eye?"

"I've got the eye," Deino said.

"Let me have it," Pemphredo demanded.

"No. I'm looking at a frog."

"You can look at the frog later. Give me the eye."

"Shan't!"

"Gimme!"

"Ouch!"

"What happened?"

"Enyo just bit me with the tooth."

"Serves you right for being mean."

During all this, Perseus had tiptoed up behind the three old hags and before they could stop him, he snatched away both the eye and the tooth.

"What?" Enyo said.

"Who?" Pemphredo demanded.

"Blimey!" Deino cried.

"All right," Perseus said. "I've got your eye and your tooth and I won't let you have them back until you tell me where I can find your sister, the Gorgon Medusa."

The three Grey Ones sat there stamping their feet in the mud and shouting.

"Who is it?"

"I can't see him!"

"Bite him!"

"I can't!"

"What a beast!"

"If you don't tell me," Perseus continued, "I'll throw your eye and your tooth away and you'll never see or bite anyone again."

"All right!"

"All right!"

"All right!"

The Grey Ones tried to grind their teeth. But since that was impossible, they ground their gums instead.

"All right," Enyo said. "Go to the land of the Hyperboreans. There's a big cave in a valley there. You can't miss it."

"And make sure you get a good look at Medusa," Pemphredo added. "Look her straight in the eyes."

"Straight in the eyes," Deino repeated. "You'll never forget your first sight of Medusa."

Perseus gave them back their eye and their tooth and left

them, their laughter echoing in his ears. The Grey Ones were still cackling to themselves, thinking how clever they had been, when he arrived in the land of the Hyperboreans.

## Medusa

Athene had not only told Perseus how to destroy the Gorgon, she had given him the means. He now carried her brightly polished shield in one hand and his sword in the other.

He knew that he must be getting close to Medusa's cave. The valley in which he stood was filled with stone people, some trapped as they turned to run, others frozen in horror, their mouths open, the screams still on their lips. It was as if they had been photographed in the last second of their life. Their reaction in that second had been caught for eternity. One young soldier had covered his face, but then he had tried to peep through his fingers. His stone hand still shuttered his stone eyes. A local government official stood rigid with a puzzled smile, his stone fingers clutching a scrap of yellowing paper. There were stone women and stone children. It was like a crazy open-air museum.

Now Perseus saw the mouth of a large cave, yawning darkly at him. Holding the shield more tightly than ever, he climbed up the gentle slope and, taking a deep breath, entered the gloom.

"Medusa!" he called out. His voice sounded lost in the shadows.

Something moved at the back of the cave.

"Medusa!" he repeated.

Now he could hear breathing and the sound of hissing.

"I am Perseus!" he announced.

"Perseus!" came a deep, throaty voice from the back of the cave. It was followed by a horrible giggling. "Have you come to see me?"

The Gorgon stepped forward into the light. For a dreadful moment, Perseus was tempted to look up at her, to meet her eyes. But with all his strength he kept his head turned away as Athene had instructed him and instead of looking at Medusa, he looked at her reflection in the shield. Now he could see her green skin, her poisonous red eyes and her yellow teeth, all reflected in the polished bronze. He lifted the sword.

"Look at me! Look at me!" the Gorgon cried.

Still he kept his eyes on the shield. He took another step into the cave. Now the reflection was huge, the teeth snarling at him out of the shield. The snakes writhed furiously, hissing with the sound of red-hot needles being plunged into water.

"Look at me! Look at me!"

How could he find her when all he could see was the reflection? Surely it would be easier to kill her if he took just one quick look at her, just to make sure that he didn't miss . . .

"Yes. That's right. Look at me!"

"No!"

With a despairing cry, Perseus swung wildly with his sword. He felt the sharp steel bite into flesh and bone. The Gorgon screamed. The snakes exploded around her head as the whole thing flew from her shoulders, bounced against the cave wall and rolled to the ground. A fountain of blood spouted out of her neck as her body crumpled. Then at last it was over. Still not looking at it, Perseus picked up the grim trophy of his victory and dropped it into a heavy sack.

### The Gorgon's Head

Perseus had many other adventures on his way back to Seriphos and, what with his long search for the Gorgon, a whole year had passed by the time he returned. The first person he saw on the island was a fisherman called Dictys. It was this man who had discovered Perseus and Danae when they had been washed ashore at the beginning of the story.

"My dear friend," Perseus said. "Here I am, back at last. Now tell me, has the king married?"

"No," Dictys said. "King Polydectes lives alone."

"And how is my mother?" Perseus asked.

At this, Dictys burst into tears.

"Oh, Master Perseus!" he cried. "It was your mother that the wicked king wished to marry. Once you were gone, he tried to force her into his bed and when she refused, he made her the palace washer-woman. For a whole year now she's been scrubbing floors and washing socks. It's a terrible thing, Master Perseus. The king just laughs at her . . . "

"He does, does he?" Perseus said through gritted teeth. "Well, we'll soon see about that!"

Throwing the bundle that he carried over his shoulder, Perseus strode into the palace and straight into the great hall where King Polydectes was sitting on his throne.

"Greetings, sire!" he called out to the astonished monarch. "It is I, Perseus, returned after twelve long months. I bring with me the present that you asked for."

"A Gorgon's head?" Polydectes muttered. "A likely story!"

"Don't you believe me, sire?" Perseus asked.

"Certainly not," the king said.

"Would you believe your own eyes?"

"Have you got it there?" the king pointed at the sack.

"See for yourself."

And with that, Perseus lifted the Gorgon's head out of the sack and held it up for the king to see.

"That's not the . . . " King Polydectes got no further than that. The next moment there was a stone statue leaning out of the throne, a stone sneer on its stone face and one stone eyebrow raised in disbelief.

After that, Perseus could have become King of Seriphos (for the courtiers were all thoroughly fed up with Polydectes and were glad to have Perseus back); but he no longer wanted to stay there. Instead he made Dictys king and left the island – eventually to become King of Mycenae.

He gave the Gorgon's head to Athene and she magically turned it into part of her armour and wore it to terrify her enemies in battle. Dictys ruled Seriphos long and well. And as for Polydectes, he was put in the palace garden as a pleasing ornament and he is probably still there to this day.

# ORPHEUS IN THE UNDERWORLD
## GREEK

Amongst the Argonauts who had sailed with Jason in pursuit of the fabled Golden Fleece, there had been one hero who carried neither sword nor shield, neither spear nor bow. His name was Orpheus, and he was famed throughout Ancient Greece as a poet and musician. When Orpheus sang, people stopped whatever they were doing and smiled in wonderment. Wild animals became tame. Even the trees and the stones would move from where they stood in order to be nearer to the sound.

Orpheus was the son of a Thracian king. His mother was one of the nine Muses: Calliope, the spirit of poetry and eloquence. His lyre had been given to him by Apollo himself, and with the Muses as his teachers he had learnt to play music in a way that is beyond description. But if you had ever heard him, it is a sound you would never have forgotten.

After his return from the Kingdom of Aeetes (where Jason was able to steal the Golden Fleece only after Orpheus had lulled the dragon that guarded it to sleep), he decided to settle down and get married. His young wife was called Eurydice. She was a nymph whom he loved very dearly and for a long time the two of them were as happy as two people can possibly be.

But then came the day when a friend called Aristaeus came to stay and took Eurydice for a walk in the fields.

This Aristaeus was a famous huntsman, a bee-keeper and the father of Actaeon. It was a warm, sunny day. Orpheus had stayed in the house to practise a new tune. The two of them were alone.

They had reached a quiet spot where the field dipped down beside a wood when Aristaeus suddenly seized hold of Eurydice, kissed her passionately and told her that he had always loved her, that he wanted to marry her, that he had only come in the hope of persuading her to run away with him. At first Eurydice thought he was joking. Then, when she saw the madness in his eyes, she called out for help. But nobody heard. Finally she managed to break free and with Aristaeus close behind her, she raced back towards the house.

She might well have got there safely, for already Aristaeus regretted what he had done. Even as he ran after her, he shouted for her forgiveness. But Eurydice wouldn't listen. His cries only made her run all the faster, barely looking where she was going. And so it was that she failed to see an emerald snake twisting through the grass. Her sandalled foot trod on its tail. It coiled round and sank its fangs into her ankle. In her panic, Eurydice hardly felt the pain but continued to run until she became giddy. A numbing coldness spread through her body. The ground rushed up at her and the light of the sun shimmered and went out. By the time Aristaeus caught up with her, she was dead.

When Orpheus was told what had happened, a terrible pallor came into his face as though part of him had died as well. For three days he stayed in his house, refusing both food and water. On the fourth day he appeared again, dressed in the same clothes he had worn on his adventures with the Argonauts, his lute in his hands. It was dawn when he left the house. Nobody saw him as he walked down the path and crossed the very field where his beloved Eurydice had fallen. For many months, nobody saw him again.

His journey took him to the very edge of the world, through countries so strange and distant that they had yet to be given names. He climbed mountains and crossed deserts. Neither hunger nor thirst could stop him, neither burning sun nor freezing snow. He came to a great ocean and set sail in a fragile boat, trusting to the wind to blow him even further to the west. He sailed for a long, long time. He sailed until the day and the night merged into an unbroken greyness and time lost its meaning. But at last he arrived on the other side and found himself on the shores of Hades, the home of the dead.

Nothing grew there. The poplar trees that lined the shore were black, their leaves as dry as dust. The soil was barren, the land cloaked in perpetual night. Not a breath of wind touched Orpheus as he walked through the immense silence towards the single mountain that dominated the coast. He alone was alive and being alive had no place there.

He came to a pair of gates a mile high, the spiked points rising higher than the mountain, brushing the very clouds. The gates were made of black iron, with iron skulls set between the twisting bars. A brazier burnt on each side, the flames as cold as ice. Behind the gates he could just make out an enormous cavern, a great circle of darkness. This was the entrance to Hades. And it was guarded.

A dog lumbered out of the shadows, growling softly at Orpheus, with not one but three heads. Its three mouths hung open, black venom dripping over needle-sharp teeth. Its six eyes blinked poisonously. The dog was huge, bigger than a horse. Its black fur hung in knots off its deformed body as if it had rolled in tar. Now it squatted, preparing to pounce. One of the heads began to howl, the horrible sound rising to a pitch and threatening to crack open the mountain itself. The other heads snapped at the air, the necks straining, the eyes bulging with hatred and fear.

Slowly, Orpheus lifted the lyre. The howling stopped. One of the heads sniffed at him suspiciously. He began to play.

The sound was tiny, lost in that eternal wilderness, but still the dog heard it. It fell silent and the muscles in its neck relaxed. One of the heads made a last protest, barking feebly, but at once the other two turned on it, tearing at its ears and cheeks with their teeth. It yelped, then listened quietly. Orpheus continued to play, louder now, the music swelling up like a blossom opening. Never had such a sound been heard at the gateway of Hades. The dog sank to the ground. Something close to pleasure flickered in its yellow eyes. Two of the heads nodded and fell asleep. The third sighed, then joined them. Orpheus played until he reached the end of the song. By then the dog was sound asleep, its tail twitching, its three heads snoring in unison. Gently, he stepped round it. The gates opened and he passed through.

A wide, sandy road led from the mouth of the cave, sloping ever more steeply downhill with every step. The way was lit by silver flames, burning in cornet-shaped braziers attached to the walls. The further Orpheus went, the more heavily he felt the weight of the earth and stone bearing down on him. He thought he must have reached the very centre of the world when he heard the sound of running water, turned a corner and saw a river sparkling eerily as it raced through a vast subterranean cavern.

A figure was standing beside a low, flat boat and as Orpheus drew nearer, he saw that it was an old man with spectacles, dressed in a threadbare grey coat and woollen mittens. The boat was shaped like a fish with a head at one end and a tail at the other. The oars had been painted to look like the wings of a dragonfly.

"Who are you?" the old man demanded, taking off his spectacles and wiping them on his sleeve. "I wasn't told anyone was coming today – not that anyone tells me anything, of course. Wait a minute!" He put the glasses back on and peered at Orpheus with bloodshot eyes. "You're not even dead!" he exclaimed. "Really, this is most irregular. You're not dead! At least, you don't look dead." He reached out with a finger and poked Orpheus. "Yes! You're alive! Ugh! Really! Well!" And he sat down in a heap.

Orpheus bent over him. "Who are you?" he asked.

"Charon," the old man said. "I run the ferry to Hades.

This is the River Acheron and that is my ferry. But I only take dead people. It's in my contract. There must be some mistake, you know." He looked up sharply. "How did you get past Cerberus?"

"Cerberus?" Orpheus asked.

"The dog. The three-headed dog! I bet he wasn't pleased to see you."

"He wasn't."

"Well, of course he wasn't. If you'd have been dead, he'd have been delighted to see you. Happy to let you in, not so happy to let you out – that's Cerberus. Now, what do you want?"

"Will you take me over the Acheron?" Orpheus said.

"Certainly not! You're alive."

"But I want to cross all the same."

"Against the rules. More than my job's worth. Sorry. Goodbye!"

Orpheus looked at the river. He would have swum but the water was flowing far too swiftly. He turned back to Charon.

"I'll tell you what," he said. "If I can make you smile, then will you take me across?"

"Smile?" Charon sniffed. "I haven't smiled for seven thousand years – and then it was only due to a misunderstanding. If you can make me smile, I'll take you across for nothing, and that's something I never do. One obol is what it costs. One obol for a one-way ticket. But I'll take you for nothing."

So once again Orpheus lifted his lyre. This time he chose a song that he knew would appeal to the old miser, a song about King Midas whose touch turned anything to gold. At first Charon merely yawned and scratched under his chin. But as the music continued, the edges of his mouth began to twitch. He shook his head and pretended to pick his teeth, but it was useless. When Orpheus sang how King Midas almost starved because all his food turned to gold before he could eat it, Charon let out a sound that was something between a grunt and a cough and smiled from ear to ear.

"And now you must keep your promise," Orpheus said when he had finished.

"All right!" The smile faded rapidly from Charon's lips. "You win. But it'll cost you one obol."

"You said you'd take me for nothing," Orpheus reminded him.

"Did I? I must have been mad. And you didn't make me smile all that much. A grin, perhaps. A mere simper. But if you insist . . ."

The old man moaned a great deal more, but he did take Orpheus across the river in his boat. He was still muttering to himself after he had dropped his passenger on the other side and was making the journey back.

"It was only a smirk, really. A nervous twitch. A wobble . . ."

Meanwhile, Orpheus continued along the path, leaving the River Acheron behind him. It was strange, for although he had descended many miles into the bowels of the earth, he now seemed to be outside again. He could see clouds above him where there should have been rock and the landscape, lit by a mysterious grey light, stretched far away to a distant horizon. He could just make out what looked like a castle on the very edge of the plateau and turned his steps in that direction.

Many were the strange sights he passed. Deep valleys crawling with strange hellish creatures. Further on, there was a man standing in a river beneath a fruit tree whose branches were heavy with sweet-smelling apples. The man was called Tantalus. Once he had been a king and had invited the gods to a cannibal feast. Now he suffered eternal hunger and thirst in Hades. For when he tried to reach the water to drink, it flowed away from his cupped hands. When he tried to pick the fruit, the branches lifted just out of his reach. Now he was a skeleton, his bones glistening behind his transparent skin.

There was the giant Tityus, stretched out on the ground, his arms and legs securely fastened. He had once attempted to make love to the mother of Zeus and had been cruelly punished for his presumption. Every day two vultures landed on him, tore out his liver and ate it raw while the giant screamed in endless agony.

There was Sisyphus who had betrayed Zeus and was now forced to push a huge stone up a steep hill, only to see it slip through his hands and roll all the way back to the bottom whenever he got anywhere near the top. There was

Ixion, spinning in the air on a burning wheel because he had tried to seduce Hera, the queen of the gods. And there were the Danaides, fifty women who had all killed their husbands. They had been condemned to fill a bottomless barrel with sand, a task that would take them to the end of time.

Orpheus saw many sights as cruel and as strange as these before he finally reached the castle. The doors opened as he approached and he passed through into a circular chamber paved with black marble, bare but for two silver thrones. A man and a woman sat facing him. Both were dressed in black, their skin as pale as ivory, their eyes hidden behind masks of shadow.

"Who are you?" the man demanded. His voice echoed in the empty chamber.

"My name is Orpheus."

"Do you know who I am?"

"No."

The man raised a hand. His fingers were long and elegant. "I am Hades, King of the Underworld. And beside me is my lady wife, Persephone. It is rare for one who is alive to come into our presence. If that life is precious to you, tell us your purpose here in the Underworld."

"I have come for my wife," Orpheus said.

"Your wife?"

"The nymph, Eurydice. For many years we lived together, happily married. Then a snake bit her. Death took her from me, but I have come to claim her back."

"That is impossible." Hades's words rang out irrevocably. "None has ever left our kingdom."

"Your majesty," Orpheus pleaded, "I have travelled to the very extremities of the world and have crossed the last ocean to reach your land. I have suffered many hardships and sacrificed many years of my life. I have confronted Cerberus, argued with Charon and endured the sight of much pain in the land around this castle. Now, I beg you, give me what I have come for: Eurydice . . . I love her."

"Love?" Hades's voice was cold. "What is love? Tell me about love, Orpheus. For how can love mean anything to death?"

"Very well, your majesty," Orpheus said. "I will tell you about love."

For a third time, Orpheus played his lyre, singing about love. And although the king's face remained as emotionless as a statue, Persephone was less able to hide her feelings. When Orpheus finished, her cheeks were wet with tears and she leant over to whisper to her husband.

"Orpheus," Hades said, and there was a strange huskiness in his voice, "your music has moved my wife. And in truth, it has affected me. I am inclined to be merciful. Eurydice is near here, not in the plain that you have crossed – which we call Tartarus – but in the Elysian Fields, where her soul has been at rest.

"You may take her with you, back to the land of the living. Play your lyre and she will follow you, guided by the sound. But we make one condition. You are not to look on her until you both stand once again beneath the sun. You are not to turn round. Mark our words well, Orpheus. If you turn before you reach your world, Eurydice will be gone and you will never see her again."

Orpheus thanked the king and the queen and left the castle, playing his lyre as he went. He played as he crossed the plain of Tartarus, looking neither behind him nor at the poor victims of Hades's wrath on either side. But even as he went, he began to wonder if Hades hadn't lied to him. Perhaps the king's show of kindness had been nothing more than a cruel trick, designed to make him leave the Underworld alone. How could he be sure that Eurydice was behind him? He listened hard, hoping to make out the sound of her footfall, but all was silent.

He reached the River Acheron and his doubts grew. Charon was waiting to ferry him across but he neither heard Eurydice climb into the boat after him, nor felt it tip in the water with her extra weight. And what of Cerberus? The ferryman had told him that the dog allowed nobody to leave. It had to be a trick. If he took just one quick glance over his shoulder he would know. If . . .

But he forced himself to continue staring ahead. The muscles in his neck were hurting, so great was the temptation to turn his head. His fingers also ached, but he went on playing. He had no choice.

*"You are not to look on her . . ."*

Now he climbed the path up towards the gates of Hades. To have come so far and to lose her now would be ridiculous. And yet suppose she wasn't there? Suppose he left the Underworld and the gates closed behind him. He might not be able to get back in. He stepped out into the sun. Cerberus was still asleep. Or perhaps he was pretending to be asleep. Was Eurydice there?

" . . . *until you both stand once again beneath the sun.*"

He looked back.

The sun didn't shine on that side of the ocean. He glimpsed Eurydice, pale and entranced, no more than a few feet away from him. And then there was a rustle of wind. She opened her mouth. The wind took her and at once she disappeared, swept away like an autumn leaf.

The gates of the Underworld clanged shut. Orpheus fell to his knees. He had lost her for ever.

# THE RIDDLE OF THE SPHINX
## GREEK

"What creature has four legs in the morning, two legs in the afternoon and three legs in the evening?"

This was almost certainly the first riddle ever invented. It was told by a ghastly creature that had arrived one day outside the city of Thebes in Ancient Greece. The creature was called the Sphinx and it had the head of a woman, the body of a lion, the wings of an eagle and the tail of a snake. There was only one road to Thebes and you could not get into the city without passing the creature. And you could not pass the creature (which was also very large and very fast) without being asked the riddle.

One of the first people who came across the Sphinx was a young man called Haemon. He had been on his way to see his uncle, who happened to be the King of Thebes, when he found his way blocked. Many other people would have run away from so bizarre a mixture of bird, beast, snake and woman, but Haemon, coming from royal stock, was afraid of nothing.

"Stand where you are!" the Sphinx demanded with the voice of an angry schoolteacher. Its tail writhed in the dust and its wings beat at the air.

"What do you want?" Haemon asked, his hand falling to his sword.

"I have a riddle for you," the Sphinx said.

"A riddle?" Haemon relaxed. "That sounds fun. What is it?"

"What creature has four legs in the morning, two legs in the afternoon and three legs in the evening?"

"Well . . . let me see now. Four legs in the morning? It's not a dog or anything like that? I did once see a goat with three legs, but it wasn't alive so I suppose that doesn't count. A frog perhaps? I don't know. I give in . . ."

The words were no sooner out of his mouth than the Sphinx pounced. Using its wings, it leapt up in the air. Then its tail slithered round Haemon's neck and began to tighten. And finally, while its woman's face laughed insanely, its claws tore him into several pieces, and in seconds the road was slippery with blood — which is one of the very earliest jokes, for "haimon" is the Greek word for "bloody". But Haemon, who was by this time being devoured, did not find it very funny.

Nor did the people of Thebes. When they discovered that it was impossible to get anywhere near the city without being confronted by a horrible monster, asked an impossible riddle, and torn apart when you failed to get it right, they almost had a riot. But there was nothing they could do. It was a bad year for business in Thebes. The bottom fell out of the tourism industry. Although King Laius and Queen Jocasta — who ruled over the city — offered a huge reward to anyone who could rid them of the Sphinx, the prize was never claimed.

Of course, princes and warriors came from far and wide to chance their arm against the creature, but it could not be destroyed by sword or arrow. Its hide was as hard as iron.

Its huge claws were razor-sharp. Its wings would carry it into the air and its tail would tighten round your throat before you could blink. Some people tried to answer the riddle. As the months passed, all manner of answers were tried: rats, bats, cats, gnats and ocelots were just some of the unsuccessful ones. Every day another scream would split the air and fresh blood would splatter on the road.

Eventually the situation became so bad that the king decided he would have to do something about it himself.

"If only we knew why this horrible creature was here," he said, "we might be able to find a way to get rid of it."

"Why not ask the Oracle?" Queen Jocasta suggested.

The Oracle was the name given to a priestess who could not only tell the future but who could answer any question put to her. As soon as the queen had mentioned it, Laius wondered why he had never thought of the Oracle himself.

"An excellent idea, my dear," he said. "I'll set off at once."

Now had King Laius ever reached the Oracle, he would have had a nasty shock. For the truth of the matter was that it was entirely his own fault that the Sphinx was there – even if he didn't know it.

A short while before, Laius had gone to stay with a friend of his and had taken a fancy to the friend's son. In fact, he had gone so far as to carry off the boy, Chrysippus, and keep him locked up as a servant in his palace at Thebes. Eventually Chrysippus had killed himself, and that might have been that, had not the entire episode been witnessed by Hera, the queen of the gods. It was to punish King Laius that she had sent the Sphinx to Thebes.

But King Laius never reached the Oracle and never found this out. For driving along the road in his chariot, he came across a young man who was actually on his way to Thebes to challenge the Sphinx. It was a narrow road and there wasn't enough room for the two of them to pass. They exchanged angry words. Then King Laius drove his chariot over the young man's foot. The young man, who had a rather violent temper, responded by hurling his spear through the king's stomach before continuing on his way.

The young man was called Oedipus. He was a rather complex character. He was not really a bad man, despite his temper. He genuinely wanted to be a hero but didn't know how to go about it. Anyway, he now turned up outside the city of Thebes and confronted the Sphinx.

"Stand where you are!" the Sphinx cried. "And tell me – if you value your life – what creature has four legs in the morning, two legs in the afternoon and three legs in the evening?"

Oedipus thought about it while the Sphinx licked its lips and practised curling and uncurling its claws. But this time it was not to be so lucky.

"I have it," Oedipus said at last. "The answer is man. For in the morning, when he is a baby, he crawls on all fours. In the afternoon of his life, he walks upright on two legs. And when he is old, in the evening, he walks with the aid of a stick."

When the Sphinx heard that its riddle had at last been guessed, it went red with anger. Its woman's head screamed, its lion's body writhed, the feathers fell out of its eagle's wings and its serpent's tail shrivelled up. Then it leapt into the air and exploded and that was the end of it.

As for Oedipus, he was given the crown of Thebes as his reward and married Queen Jocasta. He never suspected for a single minute that she was in actual fact his long-lost mother and that it was his father whom he had killed on the road . . .

But that is very definitely another story.

# PROCRUSTES AND HIS MAGIC BED
GREEK

Probably one of the most dangerous roads that wound its way through Ancient Greece, or through any other part of the world for that matter, was the coastal road between Troezen and Athens. Certainly no road ever claimed more lives. And yet to look at, it could not have appeared more safe. There were no sharp corners, no crumbling precipices over which an unsuspecting chariot might plummet. The surface was smooth and fairly well maintained. There wasn't even that much traffic, so the chances of a collision or something like that were small.

Why was it, then, that very few of the people who set out from Troezen ever actually arrived at Athens? Why was it that less than half the people leaving Athens ever made it to Troezen?

There were at least five answers to these questions, and none of them were very pleasant ones.

For the road was inhabited along virtually the whole of its length by the most ferocious bandits and the most demented killers you could possibly imagine. There were so many of them that it's amazing that anyone ever dared go that way.

First there was Periphetes, who had the charming nickname of the "cudgel-man", this referring to the enormous club with which he broke travellers' skulls. Then there was Sinis, the pine-bender. He had got into the habit of using bendy palm-trees to catapult his victims to their death. Next there was Cercyon, whose hobby was crushing people to death in wrestling bouts, and after him Sciron, who enjoyed kicking passers-by over the edge of a cliff.

But assuming that you hadn't been clubbed, catapulted, cracked, crushed or kicked to an early grave, then you might well have met Procrustes. You would soon wish that you hadn't.

Procrustes was the father of Sinis, but unlike the pine-bender, he seemed a kindly, gentle old man, who lived in a beautiful castle just off the road at the top of a hill. You might meet him as you turned a corner and he would smile at you, and the conversation might go something like this:

PROCRUSTES: Good evening!

YOU: Hello!

PROCRUSTES: Travelling far?

YOU: To Athens.

PROCRUSTES: That's quite a way from here. I tell you what – why don't you come back to my castle for a spot of supper? And you can stay the night if you like.

YOU: Well . . . er . . . actually.

At this point you might well hesitate because although the old man smiled very pleasantly and although he didn't look as though he could hurt a fly, he would be surrounded by a number of very large and very ugly men who looked very much as though they could. Some of these would be carrying bows and arrows. Others would be armed with spears or spiked clubs. The rest of them would hold swords, daggers, giant corkscrews, iron mallets and weapons so peculiarly disgusting that they didn't even have names.

And some sixth sense might whisper to you that quite possibly these people wouldn't take no for an answer.

YOU: *(Trying to smile)* Well, it's very kind of you . . .

PROCRUSTES: Not at all! As a special treat, you can sleep in my magic bed.

YOU: Magic bed?

PROCRUSTES: Yes. I've got this amazing magic bed. It fits anybody. It doesn't matter how tall you are or how short you are, it's the perfect length for you. Isn't that wonderful?

YOU: Fantastic! Is it comfortable?

PROCRUSTES: It jolly well ought to be. It cost me an arm and a leg . . .

So you would follow the old man into the castle, and he would give you an absolutely delicious dinner with plenty of wine and as you grew sleepy you might well think to yourself that you were, after all, really rather lucky to be spending the night in a wonderful magic bed. But you would be wrong. Horribly wrong.

This is how the so-called "magic" bed worked.

At one end of the bed there was a rope and drum; at the other a razor-sharp cleaver. If you were too short for the bed, Procrustes would stretch you. If you were too long, he would cut off your legs. Either way, it was one bed in which nobody ever woke up.

Only the gods can tell how many unfortunate travellers

Procrustes dealt with in this ghastly manner. He met his own end when the great prince Theseus, son of King Aegeus, travelled along this same road on his way to Athens. It was Theseus who later destroyed the infamous Minotaur – but just to get his hand in, he cudgelled Periphetes, strangled Sinis, broke Cercyon's neck, kicked Sciron over the cliff and finally arrived at the castle of Procrustes.

Procrustes ended up tied to his own bed – although whether he had to be lengthened or shortened nobody knows.

# THE EYE OF THE CYCLOPS
## GREEK

The Cyclops was certainly a terrifying creature. It was about the height of a two-storey house with thick, curly hair, a matted (and usually filthy) beard and only one eye set square in the middle of its forehead. It was grotesquely ugly, extremely bad-tempered, inordinately violent and generally worth going a long way to avoid. All this, any good book of Greek myths will tell you. But what is less often mentioned is the fact that the Cyclops was also incredibly stupid. It was probably one of the most stupid monsters that ever lived.

There were a great many Cyclopes. At one time they had been employed as blacksmiths for Zeus, but after a while they had forgotten not only how to do the work but what the work was that they were supposed to do, and had become shepherds instead. They were shepherds for almost two hundred years before it occurred to them to go and buy some sheep. Then they took their sheep and settled on an island in the middle of the Aegean Sea, where they lived in caves, seldom if ever talking to one another. There were two reasons for this. The first was that the Cyclopes were poor conversationalists, often forgetting the beginning of a sentence when they were only half-way through. But also, if there was one thing a Cyclops couldn't stand, it was another Cyclops.

The most famous Cyclops was called Polyphemus. He was the son of Poseidon, the god of the sea, but preferred to stay very much on land, looking after a flock of sheep. Polyphemus had no friends but was on intimate terms with most of the sheep. He knew them all by name, chatted to them, milked them as gently as his huge fingers could manage and shed real tears whenever he had to slaughter one in order to make his particularly delicious lamb stew.

One day, returning to his cave after a hard day's work in the hills, he was astonished to find that he had had visitors. They were still there in fact, sitting in front of his fire and feasting on one of his sheep. There were about a dozen of them and, looking more closely, he was delighted to see that they were human beings.

Polyphemus loved human beings in his own way . . . which was cooked or raw. What he particularly liked about them was the way their bones crunched between his teeth but never got caught in his throat.

The giant's face lit up in a great smile. It was also a horrible smile, for, having just one eye in the middle of his forehead, everything he did with his face was rather horrible.

"Who are you?" he demanded.

The men had by now huddled together and were looking up at him with a mixture of horror and terror. Then one of them stepped forward.

"Good monster," he said, "we are Greeks. We are returning home having fought a great war at Troy. We stopped here to find fresh provisions for our ship and thought to pass the night in your cave."

Polyphemus scowled. He had never heard of Troy and didn't particularly like being addressed as "monster".

The man bowed low. "I am sure you need no reminding," he said, "of the laws of Zeus, which demand hospitality to poor travellers such as ourselves. And I . . ."

But he was wasting his time. Polyphemus didn't even know what hospitality meant. Moreover, he was hungry. His mouth had been watering from the moment he had seen the human beings. Now, brushing the man aside, he grabbed two of his companions by their feet, dashed their brains out on the stone floor and tossed them into his mouth. Crunch! Crunch! He shivered with pleasure as they slid down his throat. Two men from twelve left nine (or was it eleven?), and if he had two more for breakfast and two more for dinner every day, they would last him until . . .

But the mathematical sum was too difficult for him. Rolling a huge stone in front of the cave's exit, he fell into a contented sleep.

He would have slept less well if he had known just who the men in the cave were. They were, as their leader had said, Greek warriors returning home from the nine long years of war that had raged around the city of Troy, and which had only ended with the famous trick of the Trojan Horse. Their leader was called Odysseus and he was to become one of the most celebrated of the Greek heroes.

He was a king, the King of Ithaca. It was Odysseus who often claimed the credit for the invention of the wooden horse, although it had in fact been the idea of Athene, the goddess of wisdom. But it was certainly true that Odysseus had been one of the men who had hidden inside the horse, and he had fought most valiantly in the sack of Troy. And whether he invented the wooden horse or not, he was well-known for his cunning and trickery.

There seemed little he could do in his present predicament, however. The stone that Polyphemus had rolled across the entrance to the cave was far too big to move and it fitted exactly without any cracks to slip through. The following morning, when the giant woke up, he could only watch helplessly as two more of his men were seized and devoured. Then the giant left, herding his sheep in front of him, and at last Odysseus was able to set his mind to work.

It was often cold on the island and Polyphemus kept a plentiful supply of wood for his fire. Each log was the size of a small tree – indeed, that's just what many of them were, for the Cyclops often plucked up whole trees and carried them home. Odysseus ordered his men to draw their swords and together they began hacking at one of the logs. It took them hours, but by the time evening arrived, they had removed all the branches, cut the tip to a needle-sharp point and hidden the whole thing at the back of the cave.

Then the stone rolled aside, the sheep came in and behind them Polyphemus. Two more of the unfortunate travellers found themselves lifted into the air, screamed as their skulls were cracked and disappeared into the giant's mouth. But this time, before Polyphemus could fall asleep, Odysseus approached him.

"Sweet monster," he cried, "I hope you have enjoyed my two friends."

"They were a bit chewy," Polyphemus replied.

"That was probably their armour. But I was wondering, dear giant, if you would care to quench your thirst with some wine after your delicious supper?"

"What's wine?" the Cyclops asked.

"It is a drink made from grapes, oh mighty one," Odysseus explained. "By chance, I have two barrels with me here. Please be my guest . . ."

He gestured towards the barrel which held enough wine for twenty men. Polyphemus snatched it up and downed the whole lot in one mouthful.

"It's good!" he exclaimed. "Do you have more?"

"One more barrel, your greatness," Odysseus said.

"Give it to me!"

"With pleasure."

Polyphemus grabbed the second barrel and drank that one down too. But the wine was very strong and as the giant had never had alcohol before, it had an immediate effect on him. He became rather drunk.

"Washernem?" he asked.

"I beg your pardon?" Odysseus said.

"Your name? Wash your name?"

"It is Oudeis," Odysseus told him, this being the Greek word for nobody.

"Nobody?" Polyphemus repeated. "Well . . . Nobody is my friend. And because he's my friend, I'll eat Nobody last of all.

I'll eat all the others first. Then Nobody after."

And with that, Polyphemus fell into a drunken slumber.

At once, Odysseus and his remaining comrades lifted up the log they had prepared and thrust the point into the fire. Soon the tip was white-hot and crackling. The noise might have woken Polyphemus up, but because of the wine he was in a deep sleep and didn't even stir when Odysseus climbed onto his chest. But he woke up and screamed the place down when the six men drove the burning stake right into his eye, turning it round and leaving it jutting out of his forehead. The Greek warriors raced to the back of the cave as he leapt up and down, bellowing so loudly that the walls shook and dust cascaded down. The noise was so great that several other Cyclopes gathered round the mouth of the cave and demanded to know what was the matter.

"I am blinded and in ghastly pain," Polyphemus moaned.

"How did it happen?" one of the Cyclops called out.

"It was Nobody's fault," Polyphemus explained.

"You mean . . . it was an accident?"

"No! No! Nobody did it to me. I blame Nobody. And I'm going to kill Nobody on account of it."

The Cyclopes looked at one another and scratched their heads.

"If nobody's done anything," they said at last, "you must be having a bad dream. Why don't you just go back to sleep and leave us in peace?"

With that, they turned their backs on the cave and went back to bed.

The following morning found Polyphemus in a miserable state. There were no Greek soldiers for breakfast that day. He couldn't even manage a piece of toast or a boiled sheep. Everything was dark for him and he had a blinding headache. Nonetheless, he rolled the stone aside to let his flock out to pasture, taking great care to feel each animal with his hands in case any of the men tried to escape.

But this was what Odysseus had been waiting for. During the course of the night, he had tied some of the sheep together, using their own long wool to do it. Then, in exactly the same way, he had tied his surviving friends underneath them so that they hung just above the ground. And although the blind giant ran his hands along the backs of the sheep, he didn't think to feel underneath them. So that way the Greeks were able to escape.

Odysseus was the last to leave. He had chosen the largest sheep for himself, not knowing that it was the giant's favourite. And to his dismay, he found himself stopped as the sheep reached the mouth of the cave.

"My dear Penelope," Polyphemus sighed, addressing the sheep. "Normally you're the first to leave, but today you're the last. Could it be that you are upset because your master has been horribly hurt by Nobody?"

"Baaah!" Odysseus said.

"You run along then," Polyphemus muttered, and, with Odysseus breathing a huge sigh of relief, he allowed the sheep to pass.

The escaped prisoners reached their ship and set sail as quickly as they could. As they left, Odysseus couldn't help laughing at the success of his plan and Polyphemus, hearing him, hurled a massive stone in the direction of the sound, missing the ship by inches.

Odysseus laughed again and called out to the giant.

"If anyone asks who blinded you, tell them it was Odysseus, son of Laertes and King of Ithaca. And perhaps the next time strangers call, you will remember the sacred laws of hospitality!"

But Polyphemus never showed anyone the slightest trace of hospitality. He spent the rest of his days sitting in the fields with his sheep, moaning to himself. And who can blame him? For it must be said that to lose one eye when you have two of them is a great misfortune, but if you have only one to begin with, then it is nothing short of a catastrophe.

# NARCISSUS
## GREEK

Narcissus was the most beautiful young man in all of Ancient Greece – at least, in the opinion of Narcissus. The blind prophet Tiresias had once foretold that he would live to a ripe old age, provided that he never knew himself. Unfortunately, Narcissus knew himself all too well.

Every morning when he woke up, the first thing he would do would be to examine himself in his full-length mirror. He would run a hand through his long, blond hair. He would wink with one of his bright blue eyes. He would flex his muscles and smile at himself with perfect, white teeth. Then he would slip on a chiton (a short tunic) and go down to breakfast.

His parents had no idea what to do with him, for although he was only sixteen years old, he was in truth remarkably good-looking. Half the girls in the country seemed to have fallen in love with him and the trouble was, he was so impossibly vain that he broke hearts left, right and centre. One girl, for example, had sworn that she would kill herself if Narcissus wasn't a little kinder to her. His only response had been to send her a sword! The wretched girl had run herself through with it and that had been the end of her.

But it wasn't only humans who were bowled over by Narcissus. Greece was also filled with nymphs, charming spirits who peopled the rivers and springs, haunted the glades and mountains and guarded the trees in the forests. One of these was called Echo, and falling in love with Narcissus was the second bad thing that happened in her life.

The first had been to play a trick on Hera who, as wife of Zeus and queen of the gods, was not known for her forgiving nature. Echo had distracted her by singing while Zeus slipped away to enjoy himself with another nymph he had happened to meet, and when Hera had found out she'd been furious. She had punished Echo by forbidding her the power of speech, and at the same time condemning her always to repeat the last words anybody spoke to her.

So when Echo tried to tell Narcissus what she felt about him, she was only able to use his words. The result was disastrous.

She met him one day in a forest. Narcissus had supposedly gone out to hunt stags, but it was really too hot for hunting and besides he was afraid he would muss up his hair or ruffle his clothes. He was wandering down a leafy path when he saw the nymph gazing nervously at him. He yawned.

"Hello," he muttered. "I suppose you're yet another of these women who find me so very attractive."

"So very attractive," Echo replied.

"I thought so," Narcissus said. "Well, you're wasting your time, I'm afraid."

"I'm afraid," Echo said.

"And so you ought to be," Narcissus continued. "To be

absolutely honest, even if you were Aphrodite herself, I wouldn't let you come near me."

"Come near me!" Echo cried.

"Are you deaf or something? I just told you I wouldn't. Now go away!"

"Away!" Echo moaned.

Realising that her plight was hopeless, the nymph fled from the wood, tears pouring down her cheeks. She spent the rest of her short life heartbroken and alone in a desolate valley, living in a cave. Her flesh disappeared. Her bones turned to stone. Soon all that was left of her was her voice – and should you ever find yourself in a valley or a cave and call out, you will still hear her reply.

Meanwhile, Narcissus continued on his way, wondering what he should wear for supper that night and whether his hair would look even better if he parted it on the left. But it so happened that Aphrodite had heard his last remark to Echo and had seen what had taken place. And she was angry. For Aphrodite was the goddess of love and Narcissus had, by his words and deeds, made himself love's enemy. She put a curse on him by making him fall in love with himself.

Narcissus had always loved himself more than was proper, but once he had fallen under the spell of Aphrodite, he was lost. On his way home, he came upon a pool of crystal water in a clearing in the forest. It was a hot, sunny day and he knelt down to take a drink. That was when he saw what was – in his eyes – the most beautiful boy in the world. His mouth fell open. So did the boy's. His eyes blinked with astonishment. So did the boy's. He smiled. The boy smiled back. He had fallen in love with his own reflection.

The next day, his parents — who had been searching everywhere for him — found him still sitting beside the pool.

"Narcissus!" they exclaimed. "What are you doing? We've been so worried about you."

"Hush!" Narcissus whispered. A single tear trickled out of the corner of his eye. "You'll frighten him away."

"Frighten who away?" his mother asked.

"The boy," Narcissus replied. "He is so beautiful . . . and yet so cruel. For when I reach out to touch him or try to kiss him he runs away from me." He reached out and touched the surface of the water and sure enough, the reflection shimmered and disappeared. "But he comes back after a while," Narcissus continued, his voice soft and far-away. "See! There he is now. Hasn't he got lovely eyes?"

"The boy's gone mad!" his father muttered.

"Come into the house, Narcissus dear," his mother said. "You haven't had supper or breakfast and you'll catch your death of cold sitting out here all night."

"No! No!" Narcissus cried. "I can't leave him. Not ever!"

And despite everything his parents said, he refused to move. All day and all night he lay in the long grass, his head propped up in his hands, gazing silently at his reflection. They brought him food. He wouldn't touch it. His torment was all the worse because although the object of his love was only a few inches away, they could never touch, they could never meet.

At last the pain became too much for him. It seemed to him that the boy in the pool had suffered too, for his face was terribly thin and his eyes were red and sore.

"I have hurt you at least as much as you have hurt me," Narcissus whispered. His hand reached for the dagger that he wore in his belt. "I shall hurt you no more."

He plunged the knife into his heart. He screamed. The boy screamed. And somewhere, far away, Echo cried out too.

Narcissus died. And Aphrodite, taking pity on him, turned his body into a flower as a reminder of what had happened. And to this day, narcissus flowers can be found, growing wild in the woods and sprouting round the banks of a silent pool.

# THE MINOTAUR
## GREEK

In the days when Athens was not a major city but a small town perched on the edge of a cliff some three miles from the sea, when King Aegeus was on the throne and the sons of Pallas still ran riot in the streets, a strange thing would happen once every seven years. Athens appeared to be gripped by some mysterious disease. The doors and shutters would close. The children would be forbidden to play. Their parents would sit indoors, their hands clasped and their faces grim. A stranger, walking through Athens, might think the whole town deserted. There would be nobody in sight. Nothing would move. But then, as the first blossoms of spring trembled in a suddenly chill breeze, he might hear a whisper, carried by the wind along the empty streets.

"Minos . . . "

And then, if he listened carefully, he might hear a second name, a name that might well have him grabbing his luggage and hurrying on his way. Throughout Ancient Greece it was a name that could inspire only the deepest dread.

"Minotaur . . . "

### The Birth of the Minotaur

The two names were, of course, inextricably linked. Minos was the King of Crete, the Island of the Hundred Cities. He was one of the most powerful sovereigns in the world. For there was no island quite like Crete at the time. Its harbour, built to hold a hundred mighty ships, was huge, fortified by towering walls and guarded by turrets rising up at intervals and garrisoned twenty-four hours a day. The capital – Knossos – was a mass of colour and life. The Cretan people, aware of their status, delighted in finery, and the market stalls, jammed together in the narrow streets, were piled high with luxuries shipped from the furthest corners of the civilized world. Silks and satins, spices and exotic foods, ivory and jewels . . . while the sun shone, the buying and selling never stopped. And overhead, the Cretan women in their gorgeous dresses fanned themselves on their balconies, waiting for the next shipments to arrive.

Yet beneath all this gaiety, there was a darker side to Crete. And even Minos, a great king and a son of Zeus himself, could not escape from its shadow.

For many years, Minos had sacrificed the best bull from his herd to Poseidon, for Crete depended on its sea-power and Poseidon was, of course, the god of the sea. One year, however, the king had decided to hold back his best animal. It was a huge, white bull, the sort of creature that could sire a whole herd of prize cattle, and it seemed absurd to waste it on the altar. Instead, he had sacrificed his second best bull, hoping that Poseidon wouldn't notice.

Poseidon did notice and his revenge was as horrible as his anger was great. He left Minos untouched but turned his powers on the king's wife, Pasiphaë, making her fall in love with the white bull. Not knowing what she was doing, the queen stole away one stormy night to the stables and it was from this unnatural union that the Minotaur was born. Minotaur means, simply, Minos bull.

As soon as it was strong enough to walk, the Minotaur went wild, destroying most of Crete and killing many of its inhabitants. Filled with shame and horror, Minos turned to the oracle to find out how to avoid the terrible scandal that was now attached to him. The oracle told him to build a labyrinth at Knossos in which to conceal both the Minotaur and his unfortunate wife. This he did. The labyrinth was designed and built by the court architect, a man of much cunning called Daedalus. This same Daedalus would one day find himself the prisoner of Minos and would escape, along with his son Icarus, by inventing a pair of waxen wings. But now he created a maze so complicated, with so many twists and turns, so many false starts and dead ends, that no man, once trapped inside it, would find his way out.

Now Pasiphaë had given birth to several children before her disgrace. The eldest of these, and the favourite son of Minos, was called Androgeus. Shortly after the Minotaur had been incarcerated, Androgeus set sail for Athens to take part in the Pan-Athenian games which were held there every five years. He was a strong, skilful athlete and he did well, winning several of the events outright. Soon he found himself being cheered on as the favourite of the crowd, much to the resentment of the Pallantids who were then living at the court.

These Pallantids were the nephews of King Aegeus and a more surly, self-opinionated bunch would have been hard to imagine. For years they had been making themselves unwelcome, fighting in the streets and lounging around the palace. Now, jealous of the success of Androgeus, they lay in ambush one evening after the games had ended and fell on him as he walked home to his lodgings. Androgeus fought bravely but he was heavily outnumbered. They killed him and left his body in the road.

When Minos heard of this he was beside himself with grief and rage. At once he ordered his fleet to set sail and the next day, when King Aegeus awoke, he found the town surrounded. Fighting was impossible. The Cretan army completely encircled the town; and the fleet itself, anchored in the shallows just off the coast, was larger than the whole of Athens. Aegeus had no choice. Kneeling before Minos, he surrendered himself and his town to the Cretan king's mercy.

"I come in search of my son's assassins," Minos said. "Yield them to me and I will leave you unharmed."

"Alas," King Aegeas replied. "That I cannot do. It was a miserable deed and gladly would I give you the killers, but in truth I do not know who they are. The cowards remain hidden. And so we must all suffer for their crime."

"And suffer you will," Minos said. "For this is my decree. I have lost a son. A son – of a sort – will avenge him. At the end of every Great Year, which is to say, every seven years, you will send to me your seven most courageous youths and your seven most beautiful maidens. Do not ask for what purpose! Suffice it to say that you will never see them again. This will be your tribute to me for the death of my eldest child. Fail and Athens will burn."

This, then, was the situation when Athens was but a small town. Every seven years, the fourteen Athenians were chosen by a lottery and taken away by ship to Crete and an unknown death. And in Crete, while the colourful throng jostled in the streets, the Minotaur stalked its victims through the subterranean maze, a dark secret like a worm at the island's heart.

### The Coming of Theseus

King Aegeus had left his home for Athens shortly before the birth of his first son, Theseus, whom he had never seen. Now Theseus arrived at the Athenian court, his reputation racing ahead of him. For the prince, only seventeen years old, had chosen to travel on the long coastal road from Troezen, a road that was usually avoided because of the hordes of bandits that waited along the way. Not only had the young man arrived safely, he had taken on five of the very worst villains and killed them all.

His father welcomed him to the palace, for Theseus was strong, fearless, good-looking, intelligent . . . in short, just about everything he could have hoped for in a son. His appearance, however, was greeted with something less than rapture by the Pallantids. Watching him, as he stood beside his father modestly recounting his adventures on the road, they realised that their days would be numbered unless something horrible happened to him soon.

They decided therefore that it was time for an open

revolt, and so half of them marched against the town from one side, while the other half went round the back to a place called Gargettus to lie in ambush. The idea was that once Theseus, Aegeus and the palace soldiers had been forced out of the town from the front, the rest of the Pallantids would surprise them from behind. It should have been foolproof. But, unfortunately for them, Theseus was no fool.

Informed of their plans by a herald named Leos, he crept out of the city in the dead of night and took the Pallantids by surprise. In a way, their plan was their own undoing, for it was easier to destroy two bands of twenty-five men than one band of fifty. Be that as it may, by the time the sun rose that morning, the whole lot of them were dead and once again the throne was secure.

Then began a great celebration the like of which had never been seen before in Athens. Aegeus embraced his son in front of the whole town and declared him Prince of Athens and heir to the throne. Fires were lit and oxen sacrificed to the gods. Tables were set up in the flower-strewn streets and every man, woman and child, regardless of age or class, joined in the feasting. The exploits of Theseus were sung aloud by the poets as the wine was poured and the food piled high. The sun shone that day and Crete and the Minotaur were forgotten.

But as the years passed and the end of the Great Year approached, the shadow returned. With the coming of spring came the old disease, the terrible fear of unspoken things. And one day, when the blossoms were at their most beautiful, the ship from the Cretan court arrived at the coast to collect the tribute of seven men and seven women.

"The Minotaur . . . the Minotaur . . . "

Theseus had never even heard of the tribute that King Minos had demanded and begged his father to tell him what was happening. Reluctantly, Aegeus explained what had happened twenty-one years before – for this was the third time that the ship with the black sails had come to Athens.

"It is wrong!" Theseus cried. "Did I not kill the murderers of Androgeus myself? We have paid the tribute in full. Enough is enough!"

"King Minos still demands the tribute," Aegeus said.

"I will not allow it!"

"You cannot prevent it. We must pay the tribute until the Minotaur is destroyed, and that will never happen, for its victims are fed to it without weapons, without any hope of survival."

"And what does this monster look like?" Theseus asked.

"Nobody has ever lived to describe it."

"Then I will have to find out for myself," Theseus said. "I will travel as one of the seven men and I will enter the creature's cave and destroy it. Then, perhaps, Minos will be content."

Aegeus tried to dissuade him, but Theseus wouldn't listen. The unfortunate fourteen had already been chosen and now he freed one boy and took his place on the ship.

He also released two of the women and put in their place two young soldiers who, with a little make-up and dresses, could just about pass for girls. When the day came for them to leave, Aegeus gave his son a white sail.

"I am an old man," he said. "Perhaps there are not many days left to me. So should you succeed in this perilous quest, sail home with this white sail on your mast. That way I will know all the sooner that my beloved son is safe."

But it was with black sails that they departed from Athens, carried by the southerly wind to Crete. It took them just two days to reach the island and a huge crowd was waiting for them in the harbour. Minos himself was there to count the victims, to check that Aegeus had not tried to cheat him and to cast an eye over the maidens to see if any were worthy of the royal bed.

He did indeed see such a girl (fortunately not one of the soldiers in disguise) and gave orders for her to be taken to the palace. But as the palace guards stepped forward, Theseus suddenly leapt between them.

"Is this how the tyrant of Crete greets his guests?" he shouted so that all could hear. "Is this the sort of behaviour we can expect from a son of Zeus?"

At this, Minos trembled with anger. "And who do you think you are, boy?" he snarled.

"I am the son of Poseidon and the prince of Athens. And I am not afraid of you, King Minos."

Now, what Theseus had said about his birth was true. For although he was the son of Aegeus, Poseidon had once been fond of his mother – Aethra – and had told her that he would look on her first-born child as his own. When he heard this, however, Minos merely laughed.

"Well," he said, "I can't honestly say that Poseidon was exactly famous for his good behaviour where the ladies were concerned. But tell me, boy, how do you account for the fact that the sea-god is your father? If you are indeed Theseus, prince of Athens, I would have thought the wrinkled old Aegeus your natural parent."

"That is my business," Theseus replied.

"Let us at least see if you are a liar as well as a scoundrel." King Minos took off a heavy gold signet ring that he had been wearing and cast it into the sea. "If Poseidon is your father, ask him to bring back the ring for me."

Minos laughed. His laughter was taken up by the crowd until the whole harbour was filled with the sound of it. Theseus stood alone, pale and defiant while his thirteen fellow Athenians waited nervously to see what would happen.

Then, suddenly, there was a loud splashing in the harbour and a silver dolphin sprang out of the water, soaring high into the air, twisted and dived down again. As the laughter faded away, it leapt up a second time, this time actually flying in a great arc over the boat. As it went, something gold dropped from its mouth and landed at the feet of Theseus. He leant down and picked it up. It was the king's ring.

"So it seems that you are who you say you are," Minos said,

raising his eyebrows. "The more's the pity, Theseus. For you have come here as part of my tribute and tomorrow you must die." He turned his back on the Athenian ship. "Take them to the palace," he snapped.

The guards marched forward. As they seized hold of Theseus, a young girl, who had been sitting next to the king, made as if to run forwards, holding herself back only with difficulty. She had been watching Theseus with interest from the moment he had defied the king. Her name was Ariadne and she was the daughter of Minos. Now, as she followed her father into the palace, she turned back to look once again at the prince.

"Theseus . . . "

She made no sound, but her lips formed the word. And she smiled to herself.

### The Slaying of the Minotaur

She came to him that night, slipping past the guards and using a duplicate key to gain entrance to his room.

"Theseus," she whispered, once the door was safely locked behind her. "I am Ariadne, the daughter of Minos . . . "

"Then you are no friend of mine," Theseus said.

"But I want to be! I want to be more than your friend." She ran her eyes hungrily over his body. He had been about to sleep and he was naked from the waist up. She smiled nervously and licked her lips. "If you will take me . . . as your wife, I will help you kill my half-brother, the Minotaur."

"You can help?"

"Of course." She stroked his arm with her hand, marvelling at the firmness of his muscles. "I can take you there now. And see – I have a sword."

"But they tell me there is a labyrinth . . . "

"You have nothing to fear." Her lips were so close to his ear that he could feel the warmth of her breath. Now her fingers were playing with his hair. "I will give you a ball of thread. Tie one end to the entrance and unwind it as you go in and you'll have no trouble finding your way out. Oh, Theseus! You have such lovely soft skin."

"Lady," Theseus said, pulling himself away from her distastefully. He tried to smile. "If you can help me, as you say, then I will certainly do what you ask."

Ariadne nodded and, taking the sword, he followed her through the sleeping palace, dodging into the shadows whenever a guard appeared. He had been locked in a room on the second floor and now they descended two stairways, their path lit by low-burning lamps. At the bottom there was a bare corridor leading to a heavy, wooden door. Ariadne gave him the ball of thread, tying one end to the handle.

"This is where the labyrinth begins, my love," she said. "I must leave you here. Be quick. I want you so much!"

"I'll . . . er . . . do my best," Theseus said. He was beginning to think that between Ariadne and the Minotaur, there wasn't a lot to choose.

Then he opened the door and stepped through.

It was cold on the other side. Far underneath the

ground, where the sun had never shone, a damp chill hung in the air. The walls were built with huge stone blocks and even three paces away from the door, the corridor branched out in a dozen different directions. Unrolling the ball of thread, Theseus tiptoed forward. There were no lights, but some freak property of the rock had filled the caverns with a ghostly green glow.

Theseus clasped his sword more tightly and continued forward. Despite himself, he could not but admire the cunning of Daedalus. But for the lifeline that connected him with the exit, he would already have been hopelessly lost. He turned left, then right, noticing with a half smile that he was crossing his own path, for he could see the thread snaking along the ground ahead of him.

"Where are you?" he whispered to himself. His breath formed a phosphorescent cloud in front of his mouth. The air smelt of seaweed. He shivered and went on, no longer caring which direction he took.

Every passage looked the same. Every corner he turned took him nowhere. Every archway he chose led only into another identical passage. Kicking something loose with his foot, he glanced down. A human skull rolled against the wall and lay still. He swallowed hard. The immense silence of the labyrinth seemed to bear down on him.

"Where are you?" he said again, more loudly this time. The words scuttled down the corridors, rebounding off the walls.

"Where are you . . . where are you . . . are you . . . ?"

Something stirred.

He heard its breathing, then the scrape of feet on sand. The breathing was slow, irregular; like an animal in pain. He turned another corner and found himself in an open arena, surrounded by open archways. Was this where the sound had come from? He could see nothing. No. There it was again. He spun round. A bulky figure stood in one of the archways. It grunted. Then moved towards him.

The Minotaur was horrible, far more horrible than he could ever have imagined. It was about the size of a man, but a large man. Stark naked it stood before him, its fists clenched, its legs slightly apart. The creature was filthy – with dirt and with dried blood. A blue moss clung to one side of its body like rust. Despite the chill, sweat dripped from its shoulders, glistening on its skin.

It was human as far as the neck. Its head was that of a bull . . . and grotesquely disproportionate to the rest of its body. So heavy was the head that its human neck was straining to support it, a pulse thudding next to its throat. Two horns curved out of its head above a pair of orange eyes. Saliva frothed around its muzzle and splashed onto the stone floor. Its teeth were not those of a bull but of a lion, jutting out of its mouth and gnashing constantly as if the creature was trying to make them fit more comfortably. The whole head was covered with white hair. It carried a piece of twisted iron, holding it like a club.

Theseus stood where he was in the centre of the arena while the Minotaur approached him. He didn't move as it raised its clumsy weapon. Only at the last moment, as the iron bar whistled down towards his head, did he raise his own sword. There was a deafening clash as metal struck metal. The Minotaur reeled away, bellowing with surprise, for none of its victims had ever carried a weapon. Taking advantage of the moment, Theseus lashed forward, but the Minotaur was too fast. It twisted away, receiving nothing worse than a gash on one arm. Then it put its head down and charged. Many young men and women had ended their lives impaled on the points of its two horns. Their blood still clung to them in a thick coat. But Theseus had been fighting all his life. With the grace of a matador, he seemed to glide to one side, then whirled round, bringing the sword lashing through the air. The blade bit into the creature's neck, cutting through sinew and bone. The Minotaur shrieked. Then animal head fell away from human body. For a moment it stood, gushing blood, its arms flailing at the air. Then it collapsed.

It took Theseus a long time to find the strength to move but then, pulling himself together, he found the end of the thread and followed it back the way he had come. At last he reached the door and with a grateful sigh, let himself out. He was soaked in the Minotaur's blood, bruised and exhausted. But he could not stop yet.

Ariadne had been busy while he was in the labyrinth. She had freed the six Athenian men from their prison and led them out of the palace. Meanwhile, the two soldiers who had come to Knossos disguised as girls had cut the throats of their guards and released the five real maidens. Now they were all waiting on the ship and as soon as Theseus had managed to find his way out of the palace and down to the harbour, they rowed hastily away, escaping under cover of darkness.

Just three knots remain to tie the loose ends of this tale.

When Minos discovered that the Minotaur was dead, he was so grateful that he forgave Theseus the death of his two guards and the loss of his daughter. His one great guilt was at last brought to an end and with it ended the tribute of the Athenians. Never again were young men and women demanded as payment for the crime of the Pallantids.

Ariadne never received the reward that she had demanded, for, sadly, she fell ill on the journey home and although she was well looked after, she died. Or at least, that is what some versions of the story say. Others have it that Theseus broke his promise and abandoned her on Naxos, the first island he came to. Who is to say which of the two endings is the more likely?

But there was one tragic ending which nobody disputes. So glad was Theseus to be returning home safely, he forgot what he had been told by his father and didn't change the colour of the sails. Old Aegeus, watching out for him on the top of the cliff, saw the black sails when the boat was still miles from the Attic coast and believing his son to have perished, flung himself into the sea. Ever afterwards the sea was called the Aegean.

Theseus was crowned King of Athens and later on

married Hippolyte, the queen of the Amazons. He was a strong if somewhat severe ruler, wiping out virtually all his enemies without a second thought. But his actions paved the way for a secure and flourishing Athens. He was also the first Athenian king to mint money. Should you ever find a Thesean coin, you will recognize it easily. For it is stamped with the head of a bull.

# THE HOUNDS OF ACTAEON
## GREEK

It had been a long day and the sun was sinking wearily behind the mountains of Orchomenus. But if the sky was the colour of blood, it found a cruel reflection in the valleys and fields. For Actaeon had been at work. Actaeon the son of Aristaeus who invented the art of bee-keeping. Actaeon the most famous huntsman in Ancient Greece.

When the horn of Actaeon was heard echoing through the forests, then the animals would tremble and the birds would rise, crashing through the undergrowth. From first light to last, he and his friends would spread their bloody net over the countryside and nothing would escape them; not the meanest fox nor the fastest deer. And every night the fire in his banqueting hall would crackle as the fat from fresh venison dripped into the flames and the smell of the roasting meat would reach the lonely shepherds on their slopes twenty miles away.

Actaeon's cloak was lined with fur and his palace walls with the heads of his catches. There was not an inch of the place that was not covered with some kind of animal pelt and even his chairs were fashioned from antlers. But it was not for these ornaments nor for the taste of meat that Actaeon delighted to hunt. It was for the love of the hunt itself: the scent, the pursuit, the trap, the kill. The autumn time, when the leaves were turning and some of the heat had gone out of the sun, that was his favourite time of year.

Then he would invite his friends out with him into the fields, urging them forward with all the eagerness of a general rallying his troops for war.

Not one, not two, but fifty hunting dogs went with him, and every single one of them was dear to him. He treated them like children (for he had no children of his own), feeding them with his own hand at the dinner table and making sure that they were all comfortably kennelled at night before going to bed himself. Each dog had a name and a character and each dog knew its exact place in the hunt.

There was Pterelas, the fastest of the pack. Once an animal was spotted, he would race forward to head it off. There was Theron the fearless. He would hurl himself past raking claw or kicking foot to lunge at the quarry's throat. Old Ichnobates was respected for his wisdom. Should the pack come across a false scent in the wood, he would know which direction to follow. No dog was more savage than Nape. His mother had been a wolf and he took as much pleasure in the hunt as Actaeon himself. Then there was Nebrophonus the strong, Melampus the Spartan, Harpalus the spotted, Lachne the shaggy . . . fifty dogs, each with its own talents to add to the kill.

It was the end of another autumn day and Actaeon was counting the number of animals that he and his pack had slaughtered. The dogs were tired, their coats matted with blood and sweat, but their tails were high and their eyes excited. For they had done their work well. Thirty carcasses lay heaped up on the grass, blood flowing sluggishly from gaping wounds and flies buzzing round sightless eyes. Now the dogs looked forward to a well-deserved rest and to a supper of rib-bone for each one of them. Actaeon's friends, too, would be glad to get back to the palace. First they would bathe; then rest. And when the moon was out and the stars were shining, the wine flowing, and the minstrels playing, there would be a great feast, a chance to swap adventures and to tell once again all the old hunting tales.

Actaeon stepped forward and raised a hand for silence. He was a young man, in his early thirties, with fair hair and dark brown eyes – not that you could have told as much from looking at him, for he was drenched in blood from head to foot.

"My friends," he said. "We have hunted enough for one day. Let us fold up our nets and put away our weapons. Tomorrow, at dawn, we can return to the fields and, who knows, perhaps we'll even manage to beat today's tally. Thirty dead, my friends. Thirty more trophies for my palace walls. A successful hunt indeed!"

The guests began to make their way home, but Actaeon, still intoxicated by the scent of blood, decided to walk a little in the evening air. He therefore climbed back down the hill and across a valley where pine trees and cypresses were growing in thick clusters. After only a few minutes he found himself quite alone. Everything was silent. There wasn't so much as a rustle in the undergrowth.

"We have killed every animal in the valley," Actaeon

muttered to himself with a vague smile. "Or if there are any survivors, they are too afraid to move."

But then he frowned because he could hear something. Where was it coming from? He listened carefully. Years of hunting had developed his hearing to the extent that the sound of a twig breaking one hundred yards away would not escape him. And there could be no mistaking the sound he was hearing now. It was just that it was so unexpected, so out of place. It was the sound of women laughing.

He tiptoed through a clump of trees, again using his skills as a huntsman to ensure that he made absolutely no noise. Now the laughter was louder, nearer, and he could also hear splashing. There was a slight rise in the ground and he got onto his hands and knees, snaking through the dust and pine-needles.

" . . . and the scorpion stung him on the heel and that was the end of that."

Actaeon heard the woman's voice before he saw her. She had just finished telling a story and the other women – there must have been about a dozen of them – laughed. At last he reached the top of the hillock. Slowly, he lifted his head and gazed in astonishment.

There was a clearing in the wood in the centre of which was a pool of limpid water, fed by a spring that gushed out of a nearby rock-face, curtaining down over the entrance to a cave. The cave had been carved by hand rather than by nature, for it was ornamented with stone pillars and garlands. The pool was surrounded by a carpet of grass and moss. Bloated flowers hanging heavy on slender stalks sprouted everywhere and the smell of perfume was quite overpowering. The sun was now almost beneath the horizon, but pink and silver shafts of light slanted down into the secret grotto from a perfect full moon.

No fewer than twenty young girls surrounded the pool, some sitting on the bank with their legs in the water, some kneeling amongst the flowers. One woman stood in their midst, quite naked, her hands cupped to pour water as she washed herself. She was the woman who had spoken and Actaeon knew who she was even before he saw her quiver and arrows lying on the grass.

The girls were nymphs. The woman was the goddess Artemis.

Artemis was the goddess of the moon, which even now hung like a vast paper lantern in the sky above her. She was also the goddess of hunting and many times had Actaeon sacrificed to her after a successful day. But far from being pleased to see him, he realised with a surge of fear that if she discovered him there he was doomed. For Artemis was renowned for her chastity. It was well known that she had actually put one of her nymphs – Callisto – to death for daring to be seduced by Zeus. Her followers lived under the strictest moral code. And for her to be spied on, in her nakedness, by a mere mortal . . . well, it was unthinkable.

But fearful though he was, he could not tear his eyes away from the scene. The goddess, after all, personified everything he held most dear. Moreover, she was beautiful. Startlingly beautiful.

She was tall and strong, with narrow hips and long, straight limbs. And yet her flesh looked soft and inviting. Her hair, the colour of leaves in autumn, fell nearly to her knees in golden streams. At moments her face was a little severe, but when she laughed (and while she continued telling her story about the divine hunter, Orion, she laughed often), she had the most beautiful smile. She looked gentle and kind; and Actaeon was certain that no man had ever seen her like this before. He dared not stay. But he could not leave.

Why Artemis spotted him, nobody knows. Perhaps he made a noise or perhaps, being a huntress herself and an immortal as well, his very breathing was enough to give him away. But suddenly her face froze and her eyes widened in shock and outrage. The nymphs screamed and scrabbled for her clothes while her hands crossed and clasped her shoulders, hiding herself. Feeling the blood rush to his cheeks, Actaeon stood up, trying to find the words to apologise for his intrusion. No words came. The eyes of the goddess were on him now and it was as if they were splitting his head in two. He groaned in pain, clutching his skull in his hands. There was a loud cracking sound and something sprouted out of his hair. With a strangled cry, he reeled backwards, tripping and rolling over on the ground.

He tried to get up, then jerked violently as his back was seized by a sudden terrible convulsion. He felt his spine bending – snapping. Somehow his clothes had been torn off him and his whole body seemed to be covered in pine-needles or . . . was it fur? He opened his mouth and was horrified to see an enormous tongue loll over his chin, a tongue that could not possibly belong to him. He was on all fours now. It was the only position that seemed comfortable. And then it was over as suddenly as it had begun. His pulse slowed down. He breathed normally. The pain had gone.

But what had happened to him? Still on all fours he climbed the hillock and walked – or was he crawling? – over to the pool. Artemis and her retinue had gone, the grotto was empty, but he could still distinguish their scent beneath the heavier smell of the flowers – and that too was strange, for although his senses had always been sharp, surely they had never been that sharp. He looked down into the water. Then he understood.

A reflection of a stag looked back at him. For that was what he was. That was what he had become. He tried to scratch his head but found that his front leg would not reach. Artemis had turned him into a stag! It was monstrous . . . monstrously unfair. It hadn't been his fault that he had seen her bathing. She hadn't even given him a chance to apologise or explain.

He stood there for a long time, wondering what he was going to do. All in all it was rather a dilemma. He didn't know how long the goddess intended him to remain a stag, and back at the palace his guests would be waiting for him, wondering what had happened. Should he go back? No.

What would they say when a stag walked in and took his place at the head of the table?

And then he heard something that sent a wave of sheer terror crashing through him. It was a sound to freeze his blood and turn every muscle in his body to water.

It was the sound of barking.

For his fifty dogs, having waited patiently for their master to return, had come in search of him. And they had picked up a new scent in the air. The scent of a stag. The hounds of Actaeon were coming. They were coming now.

He was too frightened to think. Instead he trusted to instinct . . . the instinct of a stag. He turned, tried to run. But his legs were twisted. One caught against another and he almost tripped. He opened his mouth to shout the command that would send the pack in another direction, but no sound came out. Then he was running, breaking through the undergrowth, feeling the rhythm beneath him, faster and faster.

For the first and the last time in his life he experienced the "thrill" of the hunt from the quarry's point of view. He could not see the dogs, dared not stop to see if they were catching up. He could hear nothing above the sound of his own tortured breathing. All he could do was run, uncaring where he went. Faster! In his blind panic he smashed into a tree. The branches tore at his face. Now he could taste blood. He had bitten through his tongue. Faster! He had glimpsed a dark shape out of the corner of his eye. It was a dog. They were catching up with him. Faster! His heart was going to burst. Surely they would tire soon, forget him, leave him alone. He couldn't go much further. He was seeing the forest through a pulsating red film. Tears of uncontrollable terror were pouring from his eyes. His whole body was drenched in sweat. Faster! Faster! Faster!

But still they came, the hounds of Actaeon. Pterelas, racing ahead to head him off. Theron, homing in on his throat. Ichnobates, keeping the pack on his trail. Nape, bringing the cruelty and ferocity of a wolf to the pursuit . . .

The light of the moon was relentless. The trees stood black and rigid, like iron bars. The forest seemed to stretch on for ever. And the dogs ran, their teeth bared, their eyes aglow. They would not stop. They would never stop. Not until they had killed.

That was how they had been trained.

# ROMULUS AND REMUS
## ROMAN

There were once two brothers called Numitor and Amulius. Numitor was a king, ruling wisely and kindly over the great city of Alba Longa in Northern Italy. Amulius, his younger brother, grew jealous of him, however, and one day led an armed attack on the throne which he seized for his own. King Numitor was forced into exile while Amulius kept all his possessions – including his daughter, Rhea Silvia, whom he forced to become a Vestal Virgin. This meant that she was forbidden to marry or have children, which was just what Amulius wanted, fearing that any children might one day revenge themselves on him.

Unfortunately for Amulius, the great god Mars had his eye on Rhea Silvia, who was young and very pretty. Mars was the most revered of all the Roman gods. He was the god of agriculture, of the spring and also the god of war. If you visit Rome today, you will see the remains of beautiful temples dedicated to him.

Anyway, one night he slipped down to earth and surprised Rhea Silvia as she lay sleeping. The result of this – nine months later – was the birth of twins. They were called Romulus and Remus.

Amulius was furious when he discovered what had happened. He had the wretched Rhea Silvia thrown into the River Tiber, with the twins, locked up in a box, hurled in after her. But whereas the mother drowned, the two boys were carried away by a freak current and deposited on the shore just underneath the Palatine Hill. Here they were discovered by a passing she-wolf who decided to bring them up as her own "cubs", suckling them from her breasts and curling round them to keep them warm at night. They were fed by woodpeckers which brought them nuts and fruit and even hunks of meat, and thus they grew up safe and healthy. Since that time, the wolf and the woodpecker have always been the sacred animals of the god Mars.

One day the twins were discovered, living wild in the forest, by a shepherd called Faustulus who took them back to his house. For the first time they wore clothes and ate hot food. Faustulus taught them how to talk and then his wife taught them how to read and write. For ten years they lived there, treating Faustulus as if he were their father.

In those days, shepherds had a hard life, for the country was full of bandits who preyed on them, stealing their livestock or carrying off their food and wine. But Romulus and Remus had reached their teens. They were strong and bold and skilled in swordsmanship. And suddenly it was the bandits who found themselves under attack.

Romulus and Remus became so skilfull in robbing the robbers that soon they were feared throughout the whole country. One day, however, they found themselves taken by surprise by about thirty bandits, led by a fat, bearded villain called Josephus. They fought valiantly, killing at least twenty bandits before their swords broke. Romulus managed to get away, but Remus was captured and brought before the bandit king.

"Shall we kill him, cap'n?" the bandits cried.

"No," Josephus snarled, squeezing gravy out of his beard. "Let's carry 'im orf to the local landowner. That way 'e'll get the blame for all our crimes and we'll be in the clear."

"Good thinking, cap'n!" the bandits exclaimed and proceeded to tie Remus up with so many knots that he looked like a giant ball of string.

They brought him before the local landowner and tried to make out that it was he who had been responsible for all the crimes in the area. But despite all he heard, the landowner refused to believe them. Maybe it was something about the boy's bearing. Or perhaps it was his face . . . He asked Remus to tell him about himself, and as Remus told his story, he was surprised to see tears spring from the old man's eyes. For the landowner was none other than Numitor, his grandfather. Immediately, Josephus and the surviving bandits were arrested and that night Numitor, Romulus and Remus dined together, at last reunited as a family.

After that, it wasn't long before Numitor, helped by his two grandsons, was able to turn the tables on King Amulius, who ended up more punctured than a pin-cushion. With Numitor once again restored to the throne of Alba Longa, you might have thought that all would have ended happily for Romulus and Remus, but this, alas, was not the case.

First they decided that they wanted a city all their own and, taking their leave of Numitor, they returned to the Palatine where they had been washed up all those years ago.

But now the jealousy which began the story and which had always run in the family's blood began to surface.

"We shall build a great city," Remus said. "And I shall be king."

"Forgive me, dear brother," Romulus countered, "but surely I will be king of our new city."

"Why should you be king?" Remus asked.

"Well, it was my idea to build the city in the first place."

"Hold on a minute, my dear brother," Remus said, going a little red. "If I hadn't been carried off by Josephus, none of this would ever have happened."

"It was my idea," Romulus repeated, growing red himself. "I shall be king of the new city and it will be called Rome, after me."

"I shall be king," Remus cried. "And it shall be called Reme, after me."

"Rome!"

"Reme!"

There seemed to be no way to resolve the argument. For, being twins, there wasn't even an older or a younger between them which might have decided the matter. So in the end they decided to let the gods sort it out with an omen. Romulus climbed the Palatine hill, while Remus climbed the nearby Aventine. (And even to this day there is rivalry between those two sections of the city.)

They did not have to wait long for the omen. Almost at once the clouds folded back and six great vultures flew down to the Aventine and began to circle around Remus.

"There you are!" Remus shouted, triumphantly. "The city will be Reme and I will be king. The gods have decided it."

"No!" Romulus shouted back. "The gods are on my side. The city will be Rome and I will rule. Look!"

Remus looked up, the colour draining out of his face as twelve more vultures soared out of the sky to encircle his brother. Romulus had twice as many birds as him. He had lost.

He took his defeat with bad grace and never more was there any love between him and his brother. In fact he took every opportunity to taunt Romulus about the new city, now saying that the streets would be too narrow, now sneering at the height of the walls. When Romulus dug a long trench to mark out the city's boundaries, Remus jumped over it laughing, as if to say that Rome could be captured just as easily. For Romulus, this was the last straw. He drew his sword. It flashed through the air. And before he knew what he had done, his brother lay at his feet in a spreading pool of blood.

In this way was the city of Rome founded – in blood. And perhaps for that reason did so much blood flow through its streets in its turbulent history. But that is not a matter of myth or of legend. That is a matter of history.

# THE DRAGON AND SAINT GEORGE
ENGLISH

There are no dragons today – mainly thanks to the knights and heroes who so thoughtlessly rode about the place killing them off. This is a pity, for dragons must have been astonishing creatures; part snake and part crocodile, with bits of lion, eagle and hawk thrown in for good measure. Not only could they leap into the air and fly (a tremendous feat when you think how heavy their scales must have been), but they could also run at great speed. Not that a dragon would ever run away. Dragons were generally very brave creatures. When they were angry or frightened, smoke would come hissing out of their nostrils. When things got really rough, flames would rush out of their mouths. But there was no such thing as a cowardly dragon.

Only the Chinese understood and admired the dragon. It was often said that some of the greatest Chinese emperors had been born the sons of dragons. Dragon bones and teeth were used as medicine. A dragon guarded the houses of the Chinese gods and brought rain to the earth when the crops needed it. That is why the Chinese still fly dragon kites and honour the dragon by including paper models of it in their New Year celebrations. The Chinese really did like the dragon.

But in fourth century Palestine – when Saint George was born – dragons were more feared than admired. It is true that they did have some unsettling habits. They tended to live in rather dank and nasty caves, for example, often guarding huge piles of treasure which had almost certainly been stolen from somebody else. They also had an unhealthy appetite for human flesh, their favourite food being princesses – although any young woman would do. But they were not the only man-eating animal on the globe. It was just that they got all the bad publicity.

Anyway, Saint George was the most famous dragon-killer of all – which is strange because he never actually killed a dragon. The other strange thing is that he really was born in Palestine, even though he later became the patron saint of England.

His father was a high-ranking officer in the Roman army and for a time George too served as a soldier, under Emperor Diocletian. He was converted to Christianity at a time when the Christians were suffering their worst persecution and travelled the world spreading the gospel and doing good.

His encounter with the dragon happened at a small town called Silene. Today Silene has become known as the city of Cyrene in Libya. And this is where the story begins.

The people of Silene had lived in fear of the dragon for many years. It lived in a cave on the edge of a stagnant lagoon a few miles from the town. Now, the vapours from this lagoon would often be carried by the wind into the town and the people came to believe that the dragon was responsible for the rotten smell that seeped through their streets. So they began to feed the dragon two sheep every day in the hope that it would go away. Of course, once the dragon got used to a free luncheon at twelve o'clock regularly, it decided to settle down and stay. Perhaps it even decided that the townspeople must be genuinely fond of it because they treated it so well. Certainly it had no idea that they were afraid.

Eventually the townspeople – who really were rather daft – began to run out of sheep. So a council was called at which all the most important people and the king himself met to decide what they were to do.

"We have given the dragon one thousand of our sheep," the minister for external affairs said. "But still it won't go away."

"Perhaps it won't go away," the minister for internal affairs said, "because it does not like sheep."

"I agree," the minister for ministerial affairs said. "But what are we to give it instead?"

Then the king spoke and his face was grim.

"It is well known," he said, "that dragons like the taste of children. We must give him our children. Once a week we will feed the dragon with our sons and daughters."

The result of this edict was a frightful commotion which took several minutes to quieten down. Then the king spoke again.

"We will have a lottery," he continued. "Every child in the town will be given a number. Once a week a number will be drawn out of a hat. The child that has that number will be given to the dragon in order to save the town."

He rose to his feet. "That is my law," he concluded. "There are to be no exceptions."

Three months passed during which time no fewer than a dozen children were torn from their weeping parents, tied up and left outside the dragon's cave. Seven boys and five girls met this terrible end, the flesh picked so cleanly from their bones that the little skeletons gleamed pure white in the morning sunlight. As for the dragon, it noticed the change in its feeding. It was even a trifle puzzled. But the king had been quite right to say that it would like the taste. In fact it found children delicious. And so it stayed.

By the time George arrived, an atmosphere had descended on Silene more poisonous than any mist that had been blown in from the lagoon. Every Tuesday, the day of the lottery, the streets were so silent that if the town had become a cemetery you wouldn't have noticed the difference. Few people left their homes and those who did went about their business with a pale face, their mouths stretched in a grimace of fear, each avoiding the other's eyes. Then at midday a bell would ring. Soldiers would knock on the door of a house somewhere in the town. A great cry would break the silence. And everywhere parents would hug their children and thank the gods that their number had not been chosen.

Saint George came on a Tuesday afternoon, a few hours after one of the lotteries had ended. It didn't take him long to find out what was happening in Silene and when he did find out he shook his head, half in astonishment, half in despair. Straight away he went to the palace to find the king, and as he walked into the throne-room, he heard the following conversation:

"You can't!" the king was saying. "I forbid it!"

"But you told us to," one minister replied.

"You made the law," a second said.

"And you said no exceptions," a third added.

"But she is a princess . . . my daughter." Tears ran down the king's cheeks. "She didn't even tell me that she had been given a number. When I find the idiot who gave her a number, I'll . . . "

"The princess was not given a number," the first minister interrupted. "She took one. She wanted to be like all the other children."

"My only child!" the king wept. "You can't do it!"

"It is too late, your majesty," the second minister said. "It is already done."

Saint George realised that there was no time to waste. He left the palace without even introducing himself, leapt onto his horse and rode out of the town in the direction of the lagoon. It wasn't difficult to find. The stench from the stagnant water was so strong that he could literally follow his nose.

The sound of weeping told him that he had found the cave and that, contrary to what the minister had said, he was not too late. The dragon had overslept that day and the princess was still alive, sitting on the ground with her hands tied behind her back. Saint George got off his horse and walked over to her, and at that precise moment there was a sudden rumble from inside the cave and the dragon appeared.

The dragon was far smaller than Saint George had expected – not a lot larger than his horse. It was bright green in colour with a peculiar, misshapen body. Its wings, for example, were far too small to enable it to fly. On one wing there was a pink ring and on the other a red one. It had two rather squat legs and claws and a long, serpent-like neck. But the only really menacing thing about it was its teeth which were white and very sharp. (The most accurate picture of the dragon was painted in the fifteenth century by an Italian called Uccello. You can see it hanging in the National Gallery in London.)

When the princess saw the dragon, she closed her eyes and waited for the end. But Saint George wasn't afraid.

"Naughty dragon!" he exclaimed. "Do you really mean to eat this young girl?"

The dragon growled uncertainly. The girl opened her eyes.

"Do you not know that eating people is wrong?" Saint George continued. "It's bad for dragons. And it's even worse for people!"

Smoke trickled out of the dragon's nostrils and formed a question mark over its head.

"Enough of this foolishness!" Saint George untied the girl and helped her to her feet. Then he took a ribbon from her dress and tied it round the dragon's neck. "Let us go back to Silene and talk this over." He bowed to the princess. "I must say, lady," he said, "you will make a wiser and kinder ruler than your father. That much your actions have shown."

You can imagine the uproar in Silene when Saint George and the princess returned, leading the dragon on a ribbon. Suffice it to say that once they understood what had happened, the entire town converted to Christianity.

And so, in fact, did the dragon.

A short while later the king retired from the throne and his daughter, who had in the meantime married a neighbouring prince, became queen. The two of them ruled well and wisely for many years and it would be nice to think that the dragon ended its days in the palace gardens, a friend and playmate of the queen's children, and even — although perhaps this is asking too much — a vegetarian.

# THE GRENDEL
## ANGLO-SAXON

When King Hrothgar came to the throne of Denmark (in the fifth century after Christ), he decided to build a great banqueting hall in which he would entertain all his friends. And as he was a popular king, who had fought bravely and won many fierce battles, and as he had more friends than most kings tend to have he decided that the hall would have to be larger and more splendid than any in the land of Denmark. This was how Heorot came into being. Heorot the mead-hall, the home of feasting and of singing and of storytelling.

Thatched with heather and decorated by blazing beacons and gilded antlers, the hall would fill every day with warriors and travellers, musicians and poets. King Hrothgar himself would sit at the very end of the hall on a raised dais and sometimes his wife, the fair Queen Wealtheow, would take the seat beside him. The servants would race past the roaring fires carrying steaming plates of eel pie and roasted boar's flesh to the trestle tables that ran the full length of the room. Hunting dogs, lying on the straw, would raise their heads as the meat went past, their tongues hanging out, and by the end of the feast, they too would have been rewarded with scraps of meat and marrow bones. The mead would never stop flowing. And as the sun reached out to claim possession of the night sky, the music from the harps would still ring out across the fields along with the laughter and the chatter of old comrades at ease.

Grendel heard that sound.

Curled up in the darkness of the swamp, it heard and one poisoned eye flickered open. Softly it growled to itself. For Grendel understood nothing of pleasure and so hated it. Hatred ruled its life. It was descended from Cain – the same Cain who had been cast out of Eden for the murder of his brother. Grendel blamed all mankind for the sin of its ancestor and its own fall from grace. The bitterness of centuries ran in its veins, congealing its blood. In its every waking moment it writhed in a torment of self-pity and half-formed dreams of revenge. Now, hearing the sound, it slithered through the mud and began to limp towards the hall.

It was at that grey time between night and day when it reached Heorot. Now, at last, the revellers were asleep, intoxicated by the wine and good companionship. Grendel struck quickly and greedily. Thirty warriors were snatched up from where they lay. Thirty brave men met a brutal, cowardly death. Glutted with blood, Grendel slunk away, back to the solitude of the swamp. Even in its victory, it knew no pleasure. It had done what it had set out to do; neither more nor less.

The next morning, when King Hrothgar awoke, the sweetness of the banquet turned in an instant to the bitterness of betrayal and death. Blood was everywhere, splattered on the walls and in pools on the flagstones. Nobody had woken up, so stealthily had the Grendel come, and now they found that their clothes were stained with the blood of their friends. Bones and twisted scraps of armour lay on the floor, grim reflections of the debris of the night's feasting. At once a great cry of anger and outrage went up. Spears were seized, swords unsheathed. But it was useless. How could they fight an enemy they could not see — an enemy they had never seen?

Twice more the Grendel came to Heorot, each time returning in the twilight hours to claim another thirty Danish warriors. After that, the hall was closed, and with the booming of the door it was as if all happiness had come to an end in the reign of King Hrothgar. A shadow had fallen not only across Heorot but across the whole country, and the emptiness of the banqueting hall soon came to be a fitting image for the hollowness in the heart of all Denmark.

Sometimes, King Hrothgar would return alone to his beloved Heorot. He would sit on his raised dais, drawing patterns in the dust with one finger. Then he would search with his eyes to see memories of firelight in the darkness and strain with his ears to hear echoes of laughter in the silence. He was an old man now. Twelve whole winters had passed since the Grendel had come to plague him.

It was at Heorot that he met Beowulf.

He was sitting in his chair, muttering to himself, when the door of the banqueting hall crashed open. He squinted as bright sunlight flooded in, capturing a million motes of dust within its golden beams. A figure stepped forward, silhouetted against the light which could almost have been emanating from his own body. The dust formed a shimmering aura around him. The king trembled. Never had he seen a warrior so tall, so strong.

The stranger approached and fell onto one knee. He was dressed in a blue cloak over a silvery mail-shirt. In one hand he carried a richly decorated shield, in the other a spear. His helmet masked his face but it could not hide the fair hair that tumbled down onto his shoulders, nor the bright blue eyes that shone despite the shadows.

"Your majesty!" the figure said.

"Who are you?" Hrothgar demanded, recovering himself.

"My name is Beowulf," the warrior replied. "I come from the land of the Geats. I have crossed a great sea to come before you, to serve you. And I do not come alone."

There was a movement at the door and fourteen more men entered the hall, bringing with them – or so it seemed to the old king – the light that had for so long been absent. As one they knelt before him, forming a semi-circle around his throne.

"We are soldiers of King Hygelac," Beowulf continued. "My noble father was Edgetheow, a famous fighter amongst the Geats. I too have found fame in my lifetime, and seek to add to that fame by destroying the beast that has emptied this most stately hall. My own sovereign, ever a friend of the Danes, bids me wish all health to your majesty. He too will be glad to see this monster die."

"Noble Beowulf!" the king replied. "Well is your name known to me – and that of your father. I bid you welcome. But this creature has already taken ninety of my finest warriors. I fear your quest is hopeless."

"Not so!" Beowulf said with a grim smile. "Tonight, as we feast once again in great Heorot, I will tell you something of my past exploits which will remove your fears for the present."

And so it was that the servants returned to Heorot and swept the floors and cleaned the tables and relit the beacons and fires. For that one night, Heorot relived its former glory, only this time it was not Danes who filled and refilled their goblets, but Geats. This time the stories were all tales of the exploits of Beowulf, how he had enslaved the five giants and destroyed the seething mass of sea-serpents.

"Your monster comes here unarmed," he told King Hrothgar, "so unarmed will I fight it. Yes! Neither sword nor spear will I carry. With my bare hands will I fight and defeat the beast."

The Geats raised their goblets and broke out in song. The notes were carried by the wind away from Heorot, out and across the fields. Fainter now, they travelled over the swamp until at last they reached the lair of the Grendel. Once again, the poisonous yellow eye flickered open. Its brain turned the information over as though it were chewing a piece of meat. Music. Heorot. Man. It reached out with one hand and pulled itself to its feet.

In the banqueting hall, the Geats had finished eating and were lying on their rugs, their eyes closed. Only Beowulf remained half-awake. He had taken off his coat of mail and helmet and given his sword to his attendant. Unarmed, he lay beside the door, listening to every breath of the wind, to every leaf that rustled on the ground outside.

Gliding through the shadows, the Grendel came. Pushing through the mists that shrouded the moors, it pressed on towards Heorot. When at last it saw the mead-hall, its pace quickened. One scaly foot came down on a twig, snapping it. Beowulf heard the sound and opened his eyes.

The Grendel reached the door of Heorot.

At the touch of its hands, the solid wood crumpled like paper. Two flames ignited in its eyes as it stepped inside, seeing for the first time the fifteen Geats. Saliva dripped from its mouth.

Beowulf had expected it to make straight for him. But one of the young soldiers had chosen to sleep on the other side of the door and it was this unfortunate youth who the monster seized first, tearing him into pieces and swallowing them whole.

Only then, driven to a brutal frenzy by the taste of blood, did the Grendel stretch out its hands and seize Beowulf.

At once it knew that it had made a fatal mistake. Even as its claws tightened, it found itself grasped with a strength that it would have thought impossible in a human. Suddenly afraid, it tried to pull away, to slither back into the darkness in which it had been born, but it was too late. Its whole arm was frozen in Beowulf's grip. Struggle though it might, it could not escape.

It howled. It howled in terror and sobbed in pain. Hearing the sound, the remaining Geats awoke, reaching for their weapons. But although they could make out the shape of a huge bulk beside the door, it was still too dark to see the Grendel, and when they stabbed at it with their swords, somehow their blades passed straight through it, as if through a shadow.

The Grendel screamed at Beowulf, their heads so close that they almost touched. The monster that had never once in its life known fear had now discovered terror. It had to get away, away from the impossible man who still held it in a savage grip. And away it went – snapping the tendons in its own shoulder, unlocking the bones and tearing the skin. Howling with pain, it fled from Heorot, back into the night, blood gushing from the horrible wound that it had inflicted on itself.

And inside the hall, Beowulf held the dreadful trophy of his victory. It was the monster's hand, its arm, its entire torn-off shoulder. These he hung beneath the gable of the roof. Heorot was cleansed. Never again would the creature return.

For the Grendel was dying. Even as it fled, sobbing, through the night, its life-blood was flowing out of it. By the time it reached its home in the swamp, it was cold, colder than it had ever been before. Tears flowed from its eyes as it buried its raw, jagged shoulder in the mud, trying to ease the pain.

When dawn finally came it was dead. It had died miserably, alone in its lair, and its soul had been welcomed in Hell.

# THE UGLY WIFE
## CELTIC

This is a tale of King Arthur, the legendary king of Britain who ruled over the famous Knights of the Round Table. It is also about Sir Gawain, the nephew of King Arthur and the noblest of those who sat at the Round Table. It begins (as so many of these tales do) with a damsel in distress.

She came while the court was in Carlisle. Her hair was bedraggled, her clothes torn and her eyes wild with grief.

"Help me, King Arthur!" she cried. "My husband has been stolen from me and enslaved by the wicked knight of Tarn Wathelyne. Though I fought him – see how my clothes are torn – there was nothing I could do. My husband is gone! And so I turn to you, great king. Give him back to me. Slay the knight of Tarn Wathelyne."

When King Arthur heard this, he was shocked but pleased at the same time. The sight of the poor woman genuinely moved him, of course, but he secretly loved adventure and couldn't help looking forward to this new challenge. The very same day he set out on his horse. He went alone, armed only with a spear and with Excalibur, his magic sword, and as he went he whistled. For King Arthur had never known fear – or if he had, he had never shown it.

But this time something very strange happened. As he rode further and further into a wood (which became steadily darker and darker), the whistle died on his lips. He passed a lake as black as blood on a moonless night and his whole body shivered. All the trees had lost their leaves. Their branches writhed like snakes in the wind and ragged crows hung above them, laughing in the horrible way that crows do. King Arthur's teeth began to chatter. At last he saw the knight's castle. It was vast, wider at the top than at the bottom, with two dark windows high up and a solid black portcullis below. From a distance you could have mistaken it for an enormous human skull. It was as much as King Arthur could do to point his horse towards the drawbridge. But when the portcullis opened with a loud metallic creaking and the knight of Tarn Wathelyne rode out, the last of his courage left him. With a groan, he fell to the ground, almost fainting with fear.

The knight, invisible in his black armour, dismounted from his horse and walked over to where Arthur knelt. The king could not find the strength to look up. He heard the crunch of footsteps on gravel and the clink of armour. Then came the sound of metal scraping against metal as the knight drew out his sword. There was a minute's silence that seemed to drag on for an hour. Finally came a voice as cold as death itself.

"So this is the great King Arthur!" it whispered. "Tell me – king – why should I not lop off your head while you grovel before me?"

"You . . . are . . . the . . . devil!" King Arthur gasped.

"No!" The knight laughed. "My name is Gromer Somer Joure and I am the servant of Queen Morgan le Fay, your sworn enemy. But see – the lady is here, with me."

With an effort, King Arthur raised his head and there, standing beside the knight was the woman who had sent him on the quest in the first place. But now she was smiling malevolently at him. Morgan had magically disguised herself and even in his fear, King Arthur trembled with anger at how easily he had been deceived.

"Have pity on me!" he cried.

"Killing you now would be too easy," the knight replied. "So instead I will send you on a quest. Swear to me that you will return here, on your own, exactly one year from now. But when you come back, you must answer me this question. What is it that women want most in the world? If you can give me the correct answer, I will spare your miserable life. But if you are wrong, then, King Arthur, you will die. You will die slowly – and your bones will decorate my castle walls."

The knight laughed. The lady laughed. Then they moved away. The portcullis came crashing down and King Arthur was left alone.

### The Answer

"It was sorcery, my lord," Gawain cried when he heard this story. "It was black magic. That was what caused your fear. That is what made you cry for pity. By your leave, I will ride out to the castle and . . ."

"No, my dear Gawain," King Arthur stopped him. "I have been sent on a quest. I am honour-bound. What is it that women most desire in this world? I have a year to find out."

"Then I will come with you," Gawain said. "Maybe together we'll have more luck."

So together they left Carlisle and rode out across the country, stopping every woman they met in an attempt to find the answer to the knight's question. But they soon found themselves with more answers than they knew what to do with. Some said that women most desired jewels and fine clothes, others said a good husband and loving children. Luxury, loyalty, immortality, independence . . . these were just some of the answers they received. There was one old lunatic who insisted that all women really wanted was strawberry jam. The answers ranged from the bizarre to the banal – but not one of them seemed entirely convincing.

Time passed quickly. A week turned into a month. Another month passed, then two, then six . . . Soon King Arthur and Sir Gawain found themselves on the way back to the enchanted castle. They had a whole catalogue of answers in their saddlebags, but both knew in their hearts that they had failed.

It was on the day before they were to part company, perhaps for ever, that they met an old woman. They had stopped in a clearing to rest their horses when Gawain saw her, sitting beside a stream, reading a book. His first thought was that she was beautifully dressed, for she wore the finest materials and her whole body was covered with jewels. Then she turned her head and he realised that she was without doubt the ugliest woman he had ever seen.

She really was incredibly ugly. Her two lips, like those of a chimpanzee, met several inches in front of her nose and when she smiled (and seeing Gawain, she did indeed smile), her teeth stuck out, yellow and uneven. Her skin was the colour and the texture of rice pudding and her hair would have looked better on a camel. Her nose had been pushed into her face until it had almost disappeared and she had such a bad squint that she seemed to be trying to look up her own nostrils. Finally, she was horrendously fat – so fat, in fact, that her hands and feet appeared to sprout out of her body without the benefit of arms and legs.

But she was a woman and, seeing her, King Arthur decided to have one last crack at the question. He approached her, bowing courteously, but before he could speak, she addressed him in a weird, cackling voice.

"I know the question you wish to ask," she screeched, "and I also know the answer. But I will give it to you on one condition only."

"And what is that?" King Arthur demanded.

The horrible woman grinned at Gawain and ran a wet tongue over her lips.

"That knight . . ." she said, giggling. "He is young and handsome. What lovely fair hair! What delicate blue eyes! I rather think I fancy having him as my husband. That is my condition! If you will give him to me in marriage, I will save your life."

At this, Gawain went pale. He was indeed young and good-looking. All his friends expected him to come home one day with a beautiful wife. What would they say if he was coupled with this monster . . .?

But even as these thoughts rushed into his mind, second, nobler thoughts prevailed. He had a duty – to his uncle, and to the king.

"My lord," he said. "If this woman can save your life . . ."

"I can! I can!" the ugly woman crooned.

". . . then gladly will I marry her."

"My dear nephew," King Arthur cried, "I couldn't let you do that."

"You cannot stop me," Gawain replied. He fell onto one knee. "Lady," he exclaimed. "I pledge you my word as a Knight of the Round Table that I will marry you if you can save the king. Tell him what it is that women most desire – and what you desire you will have."

And so it was that the next morning King Arthur rode – alone as he had promised – to the castle of Tarn Wathelyne. Once again the sense of evil surrounded him like a great darkness, but this time he was able to ride forward with confidence, as though the answer he carried was a blazing beacon. For a second time the great portcullis ground open and the black knight rode out, his sword already unsheathed.

"Well – king?" he growled. "Tell me the answer to my question. What is it that women most desire in this world?"

King Arthur replied boldly and clearly, repeating what the ugly woman had said to him. "It is this," he said, "that they should have their will and that they should rule over men."

For a moment the black knight was silent. Then he dropped his sword and, to Arthur's astonishment, fell to his knees.

"You have answered correctly, sire," he said, "and by doing so you have broken the spell which that evil witch Morgan le Fay had cast over me. She forced me to send you on your quest. I was her unwilling slave. But now her magic is ended, I beg you, sire, let me come and serve you at the Round Table. For beneath this foul black armour I am a good man and will prove myself worthy of you."

"You are welcome," King Arthur said, and as he spoke the dread castle of Tarn Wathelyne cracked and crumbled and suddenly there was a rushing wind as the bricks and ironwork shimmered in the darkness. Then the sunlight broke through the clouds. The castle shattered, the ground beneath it heaving as if glad to be finally rid of it. A moment later it had vanished, and once again the birds were singing.

"Let us ride together," King Arthur said, and together they turned back to the court. But although the adventure had ended well for him, his heart was heavy. He had a wedding to attend, a nephew to see married. He would have given his kingdom for it to be otherwise.

### The Wedding

The marriage of Sir Gawain was an event that nobody would ever forget. The ugly woman giggled during the service and ate so grotesquely at the feast afterwards that almost as much food went down her dress as into her mouth. She called King Arthur "Warty" and forgot everyone's names. Of course, this being the age of chivalry, everybody managed to be tremendously polite. When Sir Gawain's new wife got drunk and fell over, they rushed forward to help her up as if she had merely stumbled. When she made impossibly rude jokes, they laughed and applauded. And they all congratulated Sir Gawain on his good fortune with as much sincerity as they could muster.

Poor Gawain was the politest of all of them. Not once did he let on that he had married the ghastly woman because he had been forced to. He called her "my lady" and held her arm on the way to the table. When she emptied (or knocked over) her wine goblet, he refilled it for her. And although he was rather more silent that he was wont to be, and although he was certainly somewhat pale, he continued to behave as though nothing was wrong.

But at the end of the evening, when he found himself alone in the bedchamber with his ugly wife and watched her powdering her nose and all three of her chins, it all proved too much for him. He clutched his sword. He clutched his hair. Then he burst into tears.

"What is it, my little plum?" the lady asked. "What has so upset you on your wedding night?"

"Lady," Gawain replied, "I cannot conceal my thoughts from you. You forced me to be your husband. In truth, I would rather not."

"And why not?" the lady demanded.

"I cannot say."

"Tell me!"

"Very well." Gawain took a deep breath. "I do not want to offend you, my lady, but you are old, ugly and evidently of low birth. Forgive me. I speak only what I feel."

"But what's so wrong?" the woman gurgled. "With age comes wisdom and discretion. Are these not good things for a wife to possess? Maybe I am ugly. But if so, you will never need fear rivals while you are married to me. Is this not a good thing? Finally, you accuse me of being of low birth. Are you really such a snob, Gawain? Do you think that nobility comes just because you are born into a good family? Surely it depends on the character of a person! Can you not teach me to be noble like you?"

Gawain thought for a moment. Despite his innermost feelings, he could not help but agree that the old woman had a point. At the same time, he felt ashamed. Whatever he thought of her, she had saved the life of his uncle. He had behaved badly towards her. He had not behaved like a Knight of the Round Table.

"My lady," he said. "You are right in everything you say. I have spoken discourteously towards you and I apologise."

"Then come to bed," she said. But even as she spoke, Gawain detected something different in her voice and when he turned round he saw to his amazement that she had changed. It was no fat and ugly woman who lay on his bed but a young, beautiful girl with fair skin and soft, brown eyes.

"Gawain," she said, smiling at him. "Let me explain. Gromer Somer Joure, or the black knight, as you knew him, is my brother. Both of us were enslaved by the wicked Queen Morgan le Fay. I helped the king to release my brother from her spell but only the kindness and understanding of a noble spirit could save me from my horrible enchantment. That is what you have given me, dear Gawain, and now, at last, you see me as I really am. I am your wife – if you will have me. But this time the choice is really yours."

Gawain gazed at her, speechless. Then he took her hand in his own and held it close to his cheek.

The next morning the court was astounded to see what had happened and the king ordered a second wedding feast so that this time everyone could really enjoy themselves. Gawain and his lady lived happily together for many years and, although nobody ever told the story when either of them was present (for fear of embarrassing them), on many a winter's night the knights and their pages would gather round the crackling fire to hear once again the strange tale of the ugly wife.

# NIDUD THE CRUEL
## NORSE

One of the cruellest kings who ruled in the northern lands many hundreds of years ago went by the unusual name of Nidud. As a small boy he had probably been the sort who pulled the legs off flies. As an old man he certainly took pleasure in pulling them off people. If you were a servant in the palace of King Nidud and you spilled a glass of wine, you might well end up being flogged to death – and you would consider yourself lucky that the king was in such a good mood. For King Nidud's cruelty knew no bounds. Everybody, even his wife, called him Nidud the Cruel. And many a long evening in the palace was spent talking (or whispering, rather) of his latest act of cruelty.

Now it happened that one day King Nidud heard talk of an ironworker who was said to be descended from the elves and who lived in a house some distance from the palace. This craftsman, whose name was Volund, was known throughout the world for the beauty and delicacy of his workmanship with gold, silver and bronze.

Like many cruel men, Nidud loved jewellery and ornaments – not to admire them but simply to possess them. And when he heard about Volund, he decided at once that the craftsman should become his slave and spend the rest of his life working only for him. So he sent his soldiers out to search for Volund, to capture him and to bring him back to the palace. And this is what they did.

They came upon Volund as he lay asleep, dreaming of Hervor who had once been his wife but who had one day turned into a swan and flown away from home. Seven hundred gold rings lay on the workbench beside his bed, each one more finely wrought than any jewellery in the world. When the soldiers saw the rings, they seized them and threw them into a sack. Then they did exactly the same to Volund. And the next thing the craftsman knew, he was standing in front of the cruel king and his cruel wife and sons.

"Well, blacksmith," Nidud said, fingering one of the gold rings, "this isn't a bad piece of work. Not bad at all."

"It is mine," Volund said, quietly. "Give it back to me."

"It *was* yours," the king corrected him with an ugly smile. "Now it is mine. And so are you, blacksmith. From now on, until the day you die, you will work as my slave, making nice things for me."

"Never!" Volund cried.

At this, the king's face grew dark with anger. There was nothing Nidud hated more than someone who refused to be afraid of him. And if that someone was young and handsome, as Volund undoubtedly was, it only made it worse. For the king was old, with bloodshot eyes, a flabby face and a drooping moustache. He was also secretly a coward. So Volund was everything he was not. And that was why he hated him.

"Take him away!" the king commanded. "And set him on the tiny island of Saevarstad where he will be surrounded by water and unable to escape."

"May I make a suggestion?" the queen asked.

"Of course, my little bundle of poison."

"Have the sinews of his knee-joints severed. That way he won't be able to walk, let alone swim."

The king and his two sons laughed heartily at this suggestion. They laughed as Volund was dragged away. And they laughed all the louder when they heard his cries of pain.

So it was that Volund found himself on a rocky island surrounded by grey sky and rough sea. They had built a house with a forge and a hard wooden bed for him, but there was nothing else there for his comfort. Although he could walk a little, it was only with great pain and anyway, there was nowhere for him to go. The island was so small that he could see from one side to the other. Nothing grew there. It was always cold and wet.

Every day, a servant would row out from the palace bringing with him gold, silver and bronze, the raw materials of Volund's work. If the ironworker had made the king something beautiful the day before, the servant would also bring food. If not, he would starve. That way, Volund was forced to work and in his palace King Nidud became the envy of all his friends as more and more priceless ornaments appeared around him.

But Volund had elfin blood in his veins. He did not despair. Instead, he dreamt of escape and in a short time he had formed a plan. He could not walk but, with all his skills, perhaps he could learn to fly. And so he began to build himself a pair of wings, with feathers made of brass beaten paper-thin and struts of solid silver. Every night, after he had finished working for the king, he would turn to the wings and slowly, slowly, they began to take shape.

The one person in the palace who took no pleasure in the growing pile of jewellery was Bodvild, the king's only daughter. She was less cruel than the rest of the family (and for that reason, something of a disappointment to her father) and had fallen in love with Volund the moment she had seen him. One day, finding an excuse, she went out in the rowing boat and came to his house while he was working on a pair of golden candlesticks.

"What can I do for you, princess?" Volund asked when he saw her.

"My ring is too loose," she said, stretching out one finger.

The blacksmith flinched when he saw it, for she was wearing one of the rings that he had crafted for his wife.

"I want you to tighten it," Bodvild continued.

"Give it to me and I will see to it for you."

Volund took the ring and set to work while the princess sat and gazed at him. If the two of them had been able to read each other's minds, they would have been most surprised.

*How handsome he is*, Bodvild thought. *His hair is so fair and his eyes so blue. Until my father had his knee-joints cut and locked him up here he would have been strong and fast, but even after all his suffering, he still bears himself like a prince. How could my father do such a thing to him? He is so young, so gentle . . .*

*I could kill her*, Volund thought. *I could revenge myself on her father by taking my hammer and striking her dead. And why not? Although she is only a girl, the blood in her veins is the same blood as that of her wretched family. Yes. I will kill her and then I will throw her body into the sea . . ."*

Clutching the hammer, Volund turned round.

"I love you, Volund," the princess said. "And I hate my father for what he has done to you."

When he heard these words, Volund smiled to himself. It was not a very pleasant smile. For he realised that Princess Bodvild had lost her heart to him and that there was no need to kill her, for she would always be his.

"Leave me," he said, quietly.

"I cannot," Bodvild wept. "I hate my parents for their cruelty. I have no family now. I have only you and without you I am lost."

"Then you are lost," the ironworker said. "For knowing who your parents are, I cannot look on you except with hatred."

Bodvild fled from the house to begin the slowest death of all – the death of unrequited love. The colour drained out of her skin and her hair turned grey. She ate so little that her bones stood out. Her voice faded away to a whisper. Soon she was no more than a ghost, wandering around her father's palace with eyes that were always red with weeping.

King Nidud noticed the change in his daughter but didn't know either what had caused it or what to do about it. He did think of whipping her to try to cheer her up, or at the very least to cheer himself up, but he never got round to doing it, because by this time he had other things on his mind. His two sons had disappeared – and although Nidud had never shown much kindness to anyone or anything in his life, he was genuinely fond of his sons.

"What can have happened to them?" he asked the queen one evening over supper. "It's not like them just to . . . disappear."

"They're probably hunting or fishing," the queen said.

"I'll have them whipped when they get back," Nidud growled. "And I'll have Bodvild whipped at the same time. Look at her! Sitting there moaning all the time. Anyone would think . . ."

"Don't upset yourself, my dear," the queen interrupted. "Here – have some wine. These are the new drinking cups that Volund has sent us. Aren't they beautiful?"

"Yes," the king muttered, taking a cup in his hand. As the queen had said, it was very beautiful, although unusually large for a cup. In fact, it was just about the size of a human skull.

"Where can they have got to?" Nidud sighed, sipping his wine.

"They can look after themselves," the queen said, lifting her cup. "They've got their heads screwed on the right way."

They drank in silence, the queen running her fingers over the new necklace that Volund had sent along with the two cups. It was a very unusual necklace having just four circular stones on it, each one about the size of a human eyeball.

"Do you like it?" she asked.

"Like what?" Nidud said.

"My new necklace. For some reason it reminds me of my

two boys. I can't wait to show it to them. I'm sure their eyes will pop out of their heads."

Princess Bodvild, sitting at the far end of the table, had said nothing throughout the meal. Now the queen turned on her angrily.

"There's no need to be so sulky," she snapped. "After all, you got a new present this morning too. A lovely brooch."

It was true that the princess was wearing a lovely new brooch although that too was a little unusual. It was made with about fifty nuggets of gold, each one about the size of a human tooth.

"You really ought to be more grateful," the queen continued. "You should never look a gift-horse in the mouth."

But despite the wonderful gifts that Volund had made for them, the three of them weren't at all happy. When the night watchman came in to report that there was still no sign of the boys, the king had the unfortunate man taken out and hanged. Shortly before midnight they all went to bed. An hour later, the storm broke.

It came sweeping in over the sea. First the wind raced round the palace, then the clouds were torn apart by a writhing serpent of lightning and finally the rain lashed down. King Nidud was woken up by a clap of thunder so loud that, as he sat up in his bed, his ears rang. It was a terrible night. Looking out of his window he could see nothing but the swirl of water flashing silver against the immense blackness of the night. Trembling, he sat alone in the chamber, his knees hunched up under his chin, his hands clutching the sheets.

There was a movement just outside the window and King Nidud whimpered. In those days there was no glass in the windows and he was certain that there was some horrible monster out there in the storm about to fly in and devour him. There was another flash of lightning and he glimpsed a great pair of wings, bright gold in colour, beating against the raging wind. He wanted to hide under the sheets, but he was so afraid he could not move. Then, with another crash of thunder, the creature flew right through the window and stood at the foot of his bed.

"Help!" King Nidud screamed. "Help! It's a monster! There's a monster in my room!"

The door flew open and the queen, wrapped in a dressing gown, hurried in.

Volund the ironworker, wearing the fabulous bronze wings which he had built for himself, the water running out of his hair, pointed a finger at the king.

"It is true that there is a monster here," he said. "It is a monster of cruelty, a monster of inhumanity. And its name is King Nidud."

The queen opened her mouth to speak, but Volund continued quickly.

"Tonight I leave you," he said. "No man will ever see me again. But before I go, I must tell you how I have repaid your cruelty.

"Your daughter's heart is broken. That was not my doing. But she hates you now, as much as she loves me, and you have lost her for ever. You have also lost your sons . . . "

"Where are they?" Nidud croaked.

"They are here, in the palace," Volund laughed. "Or at least, they are here in part. They came over to my island, King Nidud. They wanted me to make them swords of gold and so they came secretly, even as your daughter had done. I killed your two sons, Nidud, to revenge myself on you. I buried their bodies beneath the forge, but first I made drinking-cups out of their skulls, a necklace out of their eyes and a brooch out of their teeth. See what your cruelty has led to! Tonight you have drunk wine out of the skulls of your children."

Then the queen laughed hysterically as her sanity left her for ever. She screamed with laughter while the king wept and cursed. And Volund stepped back out of the window to be swallowed up by the storm, leaving the wretched couple to a life of misery and madness.

# THE DEATH OF NORNAGEST
## NORSE

You may have heard that the Vikings, who terrorised Northern Europe and England during the ninth and tenth centuries, were a cruel and barbaric people, but this is not entirely the case. Although they were by nature warlike, they also had a healthy appreciation of fine art and craftsmanship. Their swords, for example, were as beautiful as they were deadly. Their ships were as elegant as they were fast. And curiously enough, as far as the Vikings were concerned, you did not have to be a great warrior to be considered a hero. You could just as easily be a poet.

This is the story of such a man – a poet and singer called Nornagest. In many ways he was the last of the Viking heroes.

His father was a nobleman, living in a small but comfortable castle. When the baby was born, he threw a banquet, as was the custom. All of his relatives and friends crowded round the new baby making the sort of inane comments that relatives and friends always make on such occasions; so nobody noticed when the front door opened and three old women wrapped up in cloaks came in.

These women were the Norns, the most powerful spirits in Scandinavia. The oldest was called Urd and she was the spirit of the past. Then came Verdandi, who was the spirit of the present. The third, who wore a veil across her face, was called Skuld and she was the most feared of the Norns, for on her word hung man's future.

When the crowd saw the three Norns approaching the cot they fell silent, partly out of respect but mainly because they were afraid. Then Urd laid her wrinkled hand on the baby's head and said:

"I bless this child with good looks, and with courage that all men will one day admire."

Then it was Verdandi's turn.

"I bless this child with the gift of poetry. Nowhere in the land will there be a greater poet."

Finally, Skuld stepped forward.

"I . . ."

But then something terrible happened. One of the relatives, carried away by the excitement of the moment, rushed forwards to pick up her little nephew who was not only going to be good-looking but a poet too. She hadn't realised that Skuld was about to speak and before anyone could stop her she had barged into the Norn and knocked her right off her feet.

Nobody spoke. The parents of the child looked on in horror. Slowly, Skuld got to her feet. Nobody could see her face, but it was clear she was shaking with anger. For a long, long minute she stood beside the cot. Then she flung her arm out, one finger pointing at a candle that burned nearby.

"The child shall live only so long as the candle lasts," she cried. "When the flame of the candle flickers and dies, so will the life of the child."

With these words, Skuld stormed out of the room with

Verdandi close behind her. But Urd stayed behind. Gently, she lifted the candle out of its holder and walked over to the unhappy parents.

"A curse uttered in anger can still be made into a blessing," she said. She blew the candle out. "Keep the candle safe," she continued. "So long as the candle remains unlit, so will your child live in health and happiness."

Then she put the candle down and followed her sisters out.

After that, the parents called the child Nornagest which means "protected by the Norns".

### At the Court of King Olaf

Nornagest grew up and, as the two Norns had predicted, he became well-known for his good looks and much admired for his poetry. In those days, poetry wasn't something you just read in dusty books or talked about in school. It lived. With the wind rattling the shutters and the flames leaping in the hearth, Nornagest would sing of gods and heroes, accompanying himself on his harp. Even without music, his voice could somehow turn the stories into songs.

For one hundred years Nornagest travelled the country. He sang of Odin and of Thor, of the mischievous Loki and the beautiful Freya. Everywhere he went, he breathed new life into the ancient myths and legends of the Vikings. As he spoke, the furnaces of Volund the blacksmith glowed once again, the eternal city of Asgard rose out of the ashes of time and the Volsungs strode forth to renew their adventures.

But in that one hundred years, things began to change. A new religion was sweeping across Europe, a religion that declared that there was only one God. For this was the age of Christianity, and although it was taught with kindness and inspiration in some parts of the world, it was forced on the people with great cruelty in others. Idols were smashed and temples destroyed. Men and women were tortured and driven out of their homes. Slowly, the old gods began to disappear.

One of the cruellest of the new Christians was King Olaf Tryggvason, who ruled Norway from AD 997 to 1000. It was to his court that Nornagest one day came. The poet was warmly greeted and after a good dinner he set up his harp in one corner of the assembly room and began to sing. His voice was as sweet as ever because in one hundred years he had hardly aged at all.

But King Olaf did not like what he heard. He was himself an elderly man with a tuft of silver hair on each side of an otherwise bald head. He had loose, rubbery lips and the bright, watery eyes of a fanatic. He had devoted his whole life – and a great many other people's deaths – to the new religion. It was all he ever thought about. And now he heard neither music nor poetry. He heard only the names of the old gods whom he had sworn to destroy. So when Nornagest paused between two songs, the king went over to him and, sticking his chest out and fixing a superior look on his face, addressed him thus:

"My dear boy," he said, "I do enjoy a nice song after supper, but I notice that you sing only of Asgard and all that stuff. Very amusing, I'm sure, but of course nobody believes in it any more – not in this day and age. At least, I assume you don't believe in it."

Nornagest narrowed his eyes but said nothing.

"Now that I come to think of it," the king continued, "I can't remember if you've been converted to the new religion or not. Would you care to remind me?"

"I am what I am," Nornagest said. "And I am happy."

"Happy?" King Olaf cried. "My dear fellow, you would be much, much happier if you converted, really you would. I've never been so happy. Ask anyone."

Once again Nornagest said nothing, and now the king grew angry.

"Of course," he said, "you could choose not to convert. But I don't think that would be a very happy decision." He gave Nornagest an ugly look. "Not unless you think you can play the harp without fingers and sing without a tongue."

Nornagest was brave, but he was no fool. He knew that, if he refused, the king would mutilate him as he had threatened. So, nodding his head sadly, he agreed that he would renounce the old gods, forget the old myths and convert to the new religion.

"Hallelujah!" King Olaf cried. "Another soul has been saved!"

He turned and began to walk back to the throne, but

then he stopped. He had remembered the story of the candle — for after that disastrous banquet the tale had been told throughout the country. Nornagest himself had heard it from his mother, who had entrusted him with the precious candle a few years before she died.

"This candle of yours," King Olaf said, rubbing his chin thoughtfully. "Do you have it with you?"

"I carry it always, sire," Nornagest said.

"Well, why don't you light it before you continue to sing? It is after all rather dark in this corner. Light the candle."

"But . . . " Nornagest began.

"You have converted!" the king exclaimed. "You no longer believe in these stupid stories of spirits and magic candles. Light it and sing or my torturers will soon have you singing another tune!"

Nornagest had no choice. He lit the candle and as the king sat down on his throne, he began to sing for the last time. There were about a hundred people in the room. They had been enjoying themselves until the king's interruption, but the atmosphere had changed. They had all been converted too. They also had denounced the old gods, disclaimed the old legends. Now their eyes flickered from the poet to the candle and back to the poet. The wax dripped. Nornagest's voice grew weaker. A breeze caught the flame and he shivered. Lower and lower burnt the wick. Soon his voice was so quiet that it could hardly be heard.

But still he sang and as he sang he reflected on the changing world and the new order of things, and his voice was sad.

There was a soft hiss and the candle went out.

"There you are," King Olaf said. "The candle's out and the boy's still fine. What did I tell you?"

Nornagest fell to the ground.

A hundred pairs of eyes turned to the king who squirmed on his throne.

Nornagest was dead.

# THE STOLEN HAMMER OF THOR
## NORSE

What we call Thursday was originally called Thor's day, for it was dedicated by the Vikings to Thor, the god of thunder and son of Odin who was himself king of the gods. Tall and strong, with a flowing red beard, Thor lived with his father in the citadel of Asgard which could only be reached by crossing a rainbow bridge. It was said by the Vikings that the sound of thunder was nothing more than the wheels of Thor's chariot rumbling over the clouds.

Thor possessed a pair of iron gloves and a magic belt that doubled his strength. His voice was so loud that it could be heard even above the clamour of a battle and would have his enemies fainting with terror. But his most prized possession was his hammer – Mjolnir – the Destroyer. Mjolnir had been made from a meteorite that had fallen to the earth during a storm. It had been fashioned into shape by a dwarf whose skill in ironwork was unrivalled. Using his strength, Thor could hurl the hammer at a target on the other side of the world. Never did it miss its mark. Once thrown, it always returned to his hand. Every year, Thor used Mjolnir to break up the ice of winter in order to allow spring to come once again.

You can imagine, then, how Thor felt when he woke up one day to find that his precious hammer was missing. He looked under his pillow, then under his bed. He tore the pillow to shreds, then the bed to matchwood. Finally, he ransacked every room in the house, knocking down several walls with his bare fists – but all to no avail.

It was then that Loki, the god of firelight, happened to pass. Seeing Thor sitting in the street with half the contents of the house and, indeed, half the house itself scattered around him, he asked what was the matter. Now Loki was a sly, untrustworthy god who delighted in mischief. Normally Thor wouldn't have trusted him as far as he could throw him (which was actually a very long way indeed), but by now he was so desperate, he told him everything.

"Don't worry, my dear fellow," Loki said. "I'll find Mjolnir for you. I expect one of the giants has stolen it."

"The giants!" Thor's face lit up. "Why didn't I think of that?"

"I can't imagine." Loki smiled to himself, for he did not think very highly of Thor's intelligence. "You wait here. I'll see what I can do."

With that, Loki turned himself into a bird and flew out of Asgard, over the rainbow bridge and on to the frozen land of Jotunheim where the giants lived. Loki was sure he would find the hammer there, for the giants had never liked the gods and they actively hated Thor, who had killed many of their number. But he was unsuccessful. Three times he flew around Jotunheim and he spied nothing. At last he settled beside a lake where, despite the ice that floated on the surface, one of the giants was swimming.

"Having a good swim, your majesty?" he asked, for the giant was none other than Thrym, King of Jotunheim.

"Not cold enough," Thrym replied, although his skin was quite blue and his beard had frozen solid. "What brings you to Jotunheim, Loki?"

"A hammer," Loki replied. "Thor's hammer, to be precise."

At that, Thrym roared with laughter. "So he sent you, did he? Well, let me tell you something, my friend. You'll never find it!"

"So you know where it is?" Loki said.

"Of course I do. I was the one who stole it! And now I've hidden it eight fathoms underground, and only I know where."

Once again the giant burst into laughter, icy drops of water splashing out of his hair.

Loki smiled politely. "I imagine," he began, "that your majesty has some exchange in mind? The hammer is useless to you. What do you want for it?"

The giant stopped laughing. "You are cunning, Loki," he said, "and you are right. For a long time now, I have been looking for a wife. Recently I heard talk of a certain Freya, the goddess of love. I am told that she is very beautiful."

"There is none more beautiful," Loki agreed.

"Then I want her. The hammer will be my wedding present to her."

"With respect," Loki said, "I'm not sure that Freya will be too happy about marrying you. I mean no offence, but your majesty is not exactly blessed with good looks. Your majesty's nose is crooked and the boil on your majesty's chin is the size of a steam pudding. Your majesty's stomach is also . . ."

"That's enough!" Thrym roared. "If I don't get Freya, Thor doesn't get the hammer. And that's final!"

Loki returned to Asgard and found Thor, still sitting outside the wreckage of his house. Thor stood up hopefully, but his face fell when he saw that Loki had come back empty-handed. Then Loki told him what he had found out and once again he cheered up.

"That's simple, then," he cried. "We'll tell Freya and, in no time at all, I'll have my beloved Mjolnir back."

"My dear Thor," Loki sighed. "Do you really think Freya will agree to marry Thrym? He's a giant, for goodness sake! And anyway, Freya is already married."

"Oh yes," Thor said. "I hadn't thought of that. But let's ask her anyway, Loki. You never know."

"No . . ." Loki agreed.


"Never!" Freya cried.

Thor and Loki stood sheepishly while the goddess of love glared at them with remarkably little love in her eyes.

"Never!" she repeated. "Thrym is a disgusting old giant. He has a boil on his chin the size of a steam pudding. I'm sorry, Thor, but I wouldn't marry him if he was the last creature alive. It's preposterous even to think of it."

"But my hammer . . ." Thor muttered.

"Forget it!" Freya cried and slammed the door.

Thor looked sadly at Loki who shrugged. "We'd better call

a meeting of the council," he said. "This needs talking about."

And so all the gods and goddesses of Asgard (apart from Freya and her husband) assembled in Odin's palace to decide what should be done, while Thor sat waiting for someone to come up with a good idea. He listened while they debated, shaking his head when one of the gods suggested he should enter Jotunheim alone to confront the king.

"It's impossible," he said. "I am virtually powerless without my hammer. Perhaps I could defeat Thrym, but not his entire court . . . "

"I could come with you," another god suggested.

"No." Again Thor shook his head. "I cannot risk the life of my friends in such a venture. And anyway, what good would it do? If we killed Thrym, we'd never find out where Mjolnir was buried."

At last Loki got to his feet and stepped into the centre of the crowded council chamber. As all eyes turned on him, he couldn't stop a mischievous smile flickering across his lips.

"I have an idea," he said.

"What is it, Loki?" Odin demanded.

"It's simple really," Loki explained. "Thrym wants Freya. Freya won't go. But suppose Thor were to go to Jotunheim disguised as Freya . . . ?"

He got no further. With a great roar, Thor sprang forward.

"Are you saying I should dress up as a woman?" he demanded.

"Exactly," Loki replied. "You'll have to shave your beard off, of course. And your legs. But it seems to me to be the only way."

"Why can't you go?"

"Because when Thrym gave me the hammer, I wouldn't know what to do with it. None of us would. It's your hammer. You'll have to go."

"Dressed as a woman?" Thor pounded his fist into his palm. "Thor, the god of thunder, wearing women's clothes? Never, Loki! I would die of shame!"

"You do Loki wrong, my son." Now Odin got to his feet. "It is a good idea. A cunning idea. There is no shame in it."

"The giants will laugh at me, Father."

"The giants will hardly be able to laugh when you have caved in their skulls," Odin said.

"I won't go!"

"You will go! Mjolnir is not just a plaything. It is a great weapon and all Asgard relies on its strength. What will happen next spring if you cannot break the ice of winter? For it is a task you cannot do without Mjolnir. No, Thor. You will go. I, Odin, command it."

There was a long silence. Then Thor nodded.

"Very well, Father," he said. "But if anyone laughs at me, I swear . . ."

"Nobody will laugh at you," Odin promised.

But of course Loki was delighted by the whole affair. In fact the plan had been at the back of his mind from the very start, which was why he had been so pleased to help. He never actually laughed at Thor, but he teased him unmercifully, simpering at him and calling him Thora. He even offered to travel to Jotunheim with him so as to enjoy the joke to its end.

After the council meeting, Thor's hair was cut short and covered by a blond wig. His beard was shaved off and his eyebrows were plucked. His legs were shaved and he was given a white silk dress. A smear of lipstick, a little eye shadow and a garland of flowers completed the transformation. Then he and Loki sneaked out of a back door, Loki shaking with silent mirth, and the two of them set off for Jotunheim.

Thrym was ecstatic when he saw the two figures appear. At once he prepared a great banquet in the hall of his castle with a fire roaring in the hearth and the best gold plate laid out on the tables. He even put a plaster over the boil on his chin so that it would not offend his new bride. It did, perhaps, surprise him that Freya was well over six feet tall. As he took her arm to help her out of the chariot, he was a little puzzled by the bulging muscles beneath the silk dress. The way she walked, with great, manly strides, did seem a touch out of character. But Thrym was too excited to realise that he was being deceived.

As the evening wore on, however, it was impossible not to notice that something strange was going on. When the banquet was served, for example, Freya ate a whole ox, eight large salmon, fifteen loaves of bread, six plates of sweetmeats and well over thirty cakes, and drank three barrels of mead before half the guests had even picked up their knives and forks. Thrym stared at Thor, then Loki, then Thor again and rubbed his eyes.

"Forgive my asking, my dear," he said. "But is this the way the goddesses of Asgard normally behave? Even giant women can't eat as much as I have just seen you consume. Do you always eat as much as that?"

"Er . . . um . . . " Thor muttered.

"The lady Freya has been fasting for eight days," Loki interrupted hastily. "She wanted to look her best for you, so . . . so she went on a diet! She hasn't touched anything for eight days."

"How kind of her!" Thrym exclaimed. "And now, I think, to show my appreciation, I will give her a little kiss." And he leaned forward, his great lips oozing in the direction of Thor's cheek.

Thor, of course, was horrified. He sprang up, lightning flashing from his eyes.

"Why do your eyes flash so, my dear?" Thrym asked. "What ever can be the matter with you?"

"Freya is tired." Once again Loki had to come up with a fast answer, for there were at least two dozen giants in the banqueting hall and had the deception been discovered, the two of them would have been torn apart before they could say "smörgasbord". Smiling, Loki led Thor back to his seat. "She hasn't been asleep for a week," he continued. "You see, she's been so excited about coming here. Her eyes are a little red. Nothing to worry about, though!"

The answer satisfied Thrym and he gave orders for his wedding present to Freya to be brought in and laid on her knees, as was the custom. The doors opened and two servants came in, carrying Mjolnir on a silver tray. The moment Thor held it, the need for pretence was over. Standing up, he threw off the wig and with one swing of his arm, cracked open Thrym's skull. As Odin had predicted, none of the giants laughed at him. They were too busy fleeing for their lives – but without success. Every time Mjolnir flew, a giant fell until soon there were none left standing.

Thor and Loki returned to Asgard in their chariot at once. As they rode over the rainbow bridge, Thor turned to the god of the fireplace and laid a hand on his shoulder.

"This has been a strange adventure," he said, "and not one that I shall remember with much joy. Thor disguised as a woman! But I am sure I can rely on you, my good friend, never to remind me of it nor to tease me about it."

"Of course you can rely on me, my dear Thora . . . I mean, my dear Thor," Loki replied.

# THE WISHES OF SAVITRI
## INDIAN

Savitri was the name of an Indian princess whose devotion to her husband went far beyond the realms of normal human experience. For she was prepared to fight with death itself to regain her love, and although there are those today who would call her "old-fashioned" and "unliberated", in her own time she was much admired as a woman and as a wife.

When she was eighteen, her father – the old King Ashwapati – suggested that she should marry, as was the custom. He was, in truth, a little concerned that as yet his daughter had received no proposals, for she was a quiet girl who preferred to read and to study her devotions than to go out dancing and enjoying herself. But Savitri gently declined.

"My dear father," she said. "I am not yet ready to marry. First let me travel for a year, praying at the shrines and listening to the words of the holy men so that I may draw closer to the Guardian Spirit."

"But Savitri," the king replied, "you are eighteen. You are of marrying age."

"I am young enough," Savitri laughed. "When I come back from my pilgrimage, if nobody has turned up you'll be welcome to arrange something for me. But perhaps these matters are best left to destiny. You'll see. If I am to be married, destiny will find me a husband."

And so it was. Savitri wandered for a year, meeting with

holy men up and down the country. She ate the simplest food and slept under the stars. To meet her, none would have guessed that she was a princess, for she had left the fineries of palace life far behind her.

Eventually her travels brought her to a forest where she chanced to see a tall, handsome man carrying an axe in one hand and a bundle of firewood in the other. At first she thought he was nothing more than a huntsman or forester but there was something about him – the nobility of his bearing perhaps – that made her think again. Despite the roughness of his clothes and the meanness of his occupation, she could not help but wonder if, like herself, he was not royally born, and out of sheer curiosity (or at least, she assured herself that it was only curiosity) she asked him to tell her about himself.

"Madam," the young man said. "My name is Satyavan. Once I lived in a great palace, surrounded by stewards and servants. My father was the king, but in his old age, he lost his sight. Then his courtiers were able to conspire against him and – alas that I was not old enough to defend him – he was overthrown and banished. Now we live in poverty, in a small cottage in the forest. It is a hard life . . . not so much for me, but it is very hard for my poor father. I am taking him this wood now. I wish that I could bring him something that would comfort him more!"

When Savitri returned to her own palace, the joy of her arrival turned to astonishment when she announced that she intended to marry, and there was dismay when the name of her fiancé was revealed. For there was in the palace a holy man called Narada who knew everything that there was to know.

"You must not marry this Satyavan," he said.

"Why not?" Savitri asked.

"Because the unfortunate young man is living under a curse. One year from now you will be not a wife but a widow. Yes! Satyavan has only twelve months to live."

Now every Hindu woman desires to die before her husband and when the princess heard this news her face went pale. But she had already plighted herself to Satyavan and did not intend to break her word. Try though her father and Narada might to dissuade her, she insisted on going ahead with the marriage.

And so the wedding was proclaimed. An iron ring was bound on Savitri's left wrist and her veil was tied to the cloak of Satyavan, as custom dictated. A sacred fire was lit and hand in hand they walked around it seven times while a priest chanted the ancient prayers. Then she put away all her jewels and fine clothes and went to live in the forest as the devoted wife of Satyavan and the dutiful daughter of his parents.

Never once did she tell her husband what Narada had foreseen, but never for a minute could she forget it. If Satyavan had an appointment with the god of death, then nothing could come between the two of them. For it is often said in India that Yama, the god of death, is the only god who never breaks his word and that if something is absolutely certain, then it is "as true as death". For this reason, Yama is also known as the god of truth and of faith.

And after twelve months, he came.

Savitri and Satyavan were walking in the forest together. It was a beautiful summer's day, the grass a soft green beneath their feet and the sun showering them with emeralds as it broke through the leafy roof. She was carrying a basket filled with wild fruit. He, as ever, carried his axe – for even in the warm weather he liked to keep the stores of firewood well supplied. He had been working while Savitri sang to him, when suddenly he stopped and complained that he was dizzy. A moment later he dropped the axe and staggered. Suddenly cold with dread, Savitri ran to him, and she caught him just as he fell, fainting into her lap.

There was a rustle in the undergrowth and it seemed as if a cloud had passed across the face of the sun, for the glade was thrown into shadow. When Savitri looked up she saw a figure dressed in black, a noose of rough rope clasped in one hand. He looked at her with a sad expression and nodded. Then she knew that this was Yama and that he had come for her husband.

"Savitri," he said, and his voice was strangely musical, like a song in a minor key. "I claim the soul of Satyavan as is my right. Do not be afraid for him. All his sorrows are now over."

He leant down and fastened the rope around the dying man's head, his hand brushing against the flowing locks of hair that only that morning had lain on the pillow beside her. At the touch of the rope, the soul of Satyavan separated from his body, standing up to follow Yama.

"Farewell," Yama said. "And remember – I am the only god to whom everyone is faithful. One day you and I will meet again."

He turned and walked away but, driven by an instinct that made her forget her fear, Savitri followed. She followed him through the forest and into a second clearing where a waterfall splashed down into a rocky pool. Hearing her, Yama turned again and now two black flames flickered where his eyes should have been, for his head had become a skull and his body, beneath the robes, a bare skeleton. But Savitri was not afraid.

"Still here!" Yama exclaimed. "I see that you have more courage than sense, for who would willingly follow the god of death? Very well – I will give you a gift to help soothe your grief. You may ask for anything you like except for the life of your husband."

"Then I ask for my father-in-law's sight to be returned," Savitri said.

"It is granted," Yama said. "Now farewell again."

For a second time, the god of death walked away, leading the soul of Satyavan behind him on the rope. Now the forest grew wild. Thistles sprung up and thorns pressed in on the path. Wild bats flitted in the air and owls hooted mysteriously in the shadows. But still Savitri followed, and when Yama looked back, there she still was.

"I shall give you another wish," Yama said, and now his voice was angry. "It is as much to dissuade you from this folly as to reward you for your devotion to your dead husband. But once again you may not ask for his life. Anything but that!"

"Then I would like my father-in-law's kingdom and his wealth to be returned to him," Savitri said.

"It is done. Now leave me!"

But Savitri, believing herself to be almost a friend of death, followed on. The forest grew ever darker and more savage. Now strange figures could be glimpsed gliding silently between the trees. A foul-smelling swamp bubbled nearby, tentacles of white mist spreading out over the ground.

"Still here!" exclaimed Yama in all his fury when he turned round for a third time. "Never has a mortal so defied me! And a woman! A woman with the courage of ten men it would seem. Very well! One last wish will I grant you but then you and I must part company, lest I decide to keep you in my shadowy kingdom for all eternity. What will you have this time? So far you have favoured only your father-in-law. Now what can I give you for yourself?"

"Only this," Savitri said. "Grant that I may have many children and that I should live to see their children's children grow up in health and happiness. Will you give me this, great Yama?"

"It is a good wish," Yama said with a smile. "And I grant it."

Then it was Savitri's turn to smile. "You have forgotten," she said, "that according to Hindu law, a widow can not remarry."

Yama thought for a moment, realising how he had been tricked. If Savitri could not remarry, then how could she have children and grandchildren? And yet that was what he had promised her, he who never broke his word. In which case . . .

For a second, Savitri thought the god of death was going to strike her down where she stood, but then the forest rang with the sound of his laughter and he pulled the noose from around Satyavan's neck.

"It is a courageous woman who would follow her husband into the grave," he said. "And it is a cunning woman who would trick the god of death himself. Very well, Savitri. I will give you back the only man who can be the father of your children. And it will be a long, long time before the two of us meet again. Go in peace, for your devotion to Satyavan has defeated me."

Savitri and Satyavan returned to their cottage to discover that the sight and the fortunes of the old king had indeed been restored. And thus began a long and happy life in which the two were always true to one another. As true, indeed, as death.

# THE GREAT BELL OF PEKING
## CHINESE

When Peking became the capital of China, it was decreed by the Emperor, Yung Lo, that two towers should be built. One would be a look-out tower and would be furnished with a magnificent drum. The other would be an alarm tower and would contain a great bell. This bell would have two purposes. First it would be sounded should some enemy be sighted outside the city's walls. But it would also be larger and louder than any other bell in China and as such would be a fitting symbol for the new capital of the country.

Yung Lo therefore approached the most celebrated bell-maker in China, a man by the name of Kuan Yu. The Emperor explained what was wanted and gave him a purse of gold coins with which to employ a small army of craftsmen and with which to buy the necessary amounts of metal. Kuan Yu set to work at once, but it was three months before he was able to announce that the bell was ready.

At once the Emperor set out from his palace in a triumphal procession. Carried in his golden throne and surrounded by courtiers and musicians, he arrived at Kuan Yu's workshop. The bell was not actually finished, but the mould in which it was to be cast was complete and the metal for the bell was molten and bubbling. The Emperor took his place and a signal for the last stage of the construction was given. The huge vat of liquid metal was upturned. A silver river ran hissing down the conduits and went swirling into the mould. Then there was a long wait while the metal cooled until at last the mould could be cracked open and the bell revealed. The Emperor and his courtiers leant forward. The mould was peeled away rather like an eggshell. Kuan Yu went pale. The courtiers gasped. For something had gone wrong and the bell was pitted with holes. The whole thing was useless. Three months' work and a small fortune had gone down the drain.

Fortunately, Yung Lo was of a forgiving nature. He gave the bell-maker another purse of gold and instructed him to start again. Another three months passed during which time Kuan Yu worked in a fury, checking and re-checking his plans, tending the furnaces and monitoring every second of the new mould's construction. At last the time came for a second attempt. The Emperor was summoned. The workshop was prepared.

As the second silver river trickled along the conduits, nobody spoke. As the mould cooled, you could have heard a pin drop. Finally, with a trembling hand, Kuan Yu broke it open. This time he almost fainted so great was the shock. For the bell had cracked into three pieces, one for every month that had gone into its construction. Once again it was useless. Once again the Emperor's money had been wasted.

Now Yung Lo was a patient man. Many Emperors would have taken the bell-maker's two failures as a personal insult and would have had the poor man put to a horrible death. But Yung Lo did not lose his temper. He gave Kuan Yu a third purse of gold, but this time he leant forward and whispered to him.

"To fail once was understandable," he said. "To fail twice was pardonable. But even I cannot permit a third mistake."

"I understand, sire," the bell-maker quavered.

"One more mistake must cost you your life," the Emperor said. "You have three more months to finish the work. Give me my bell or die."

Once more Kuan Yu set to work, but this time it was with a heavy heart. For he had come to believe that the bell was cursed, that he would never be able to finish it properly and that however hard he tried he would still lose his life. It was in this mood that his daughter found him one evening, sitting by the fire with his head in his hands.

Kuan Yu was a widower. His wife had died of an illness many years before and he lived alone with his daughter, Ko-ai. Now aged sixteen, she was a beautiful girl with soft, almond eyes, long silken lashes and hair as black as midnight. She was slim and graceful, with a gentle voice that almost sang rather than spoke. As well as looking after the house and cooking for her father, Ko-ai was a skilful poet and a talented painter. Needless to say, Kuan Yu loved his daughter dearly.

Seeing how unhappy her father looked, Ko-ai sat beside him, resting her head in his lap, and asked him what was wrong.

"Twice have I failed my Emperor," Kuan Yu muttered. "If it happens a third time, I am doomed. And yet . . . " He turned the plans of the third bell over in his hand. "I am afraid," he whispered.

"If only I could help . . . " Ko-ai said.

"There is nothing you can do," Kuan Yu replied. "The casting of the bell is only a few days away. After that, my dear, you will be alone."

The next day, Ko-ai got up early and slipped quietly out of the house. Then she crossed Peking on foot until she came to the house of a famous magician whose name was Kuo Po. As she lifted her hand to knock on the door, it opened by itself and she stepped into a dark, incense-filled passage that led to a circular room where the magician was waiting for her, sitting cross-legged on a rush mat.

"Greetings, Ko-ai," he said.

"You know my name!" she exclaimed.

The magician bowed his bald head. "It is my business to know. I know also the business that brings you here. You have a question. I warn you — don't ask it. The answer may not be to your liking."

"But I must know," Ko-ai said, speaking in a low voice.

"Very well. The third bell will fail."

Ko-ai fell back, tears starting to fill her eyes. But then the magician raised a hand.

"The bell will fail," he said, "unless the blood of a young girl is mixed with the molten metal."

"But . . ."

"I warned you not to ask. Now you know. Only the blood of a young girl will save your father from execution. Now leave me!"

The day of the third casting arrived.

Once more the Emperor set out from the palace but this

time, as well as the courtiers and musicians, his retinue included a hooded executioner carrying an axe. For the third and last time the cauldron of metal was heated to boiling point, the steam swirling upwards, the surface bubbling and spitting. So intense was the heat that everyone in the workroom was sweating. Or was it just the heat? For fear was in the air – fear of another failure and an Emperor's wrath.

Then, just as the signal was given for the cauldron to be upturned, Ko-ai appeared, running along a gantry just below the ceiling.

"Father!" she shouted. "I do this for you!"

Then she leapt off the gantry and dived head-first into the molten metal. A servant tried to catch her as she fell, but all he caught was her shoe which came off in his hand.

Kuan Yu screamed and fainted dead away.

His daughter's body hit the surface of the metal and disappeared into it as if through some magical mirror. At once there was a great sizzling and a horrible smell filled the air.

At the same moment, the cauldron, which had already begun to slant, upturned. The metal ran out, racing down the conduits and into the mould. But this time it was streaked with red.

Nobody would ever forget the nightmare of that day. Kuan Yu had to be helped to his bedroom where he remained, driven completely insane by what he had seen. From that moment on, whenever he heard the sound of a bell, he would froth at the mouth and it would take six strong men to tie him to his bed. The Emperor returned to his palace with his stunned courtiers. Never again would his musicians be able to play in tune. Nor, for that matter, would the executioner ever manage to perform another execution, for his nerves had been permanently shattered.

But when the bell had cooled and the mould had been cracked open, it was discovered that, just as the magician had predicted, it was Kuan Yu's greatest triumph. And despite everything, the Emperor ordered that it should be hung in the tower as intended.

When the citizens of Peking heard the story of Ko-ai's heroism and saw the bell being carried out of the house by a hundred strong men, they became very curious to know what it would sound like. The bell certainly looked peculiar, for the red streaks could still be seen, swirling around in the silver. They watched with interest as it was hauled up and hung in the tower and when the day came for the first sounding, the streets were so packed that nobody in the city could move. Even the Emperor turned up for the first ringing, which was to be at midday exactly.

The sun rose in the sky. At last the moment came.

The bell was struck and indeed the sound was so loud and impressive that the Emperor really felt that he had got his money's worth. But then the crowd gasped with horror. For the boom of the bell was immediately followed by a ghastly shriek, exactly the same sound that Ko-ai had made as her hands had hit the scalding metal. And even as the scream died away, the word "hsieh" was heard, whispered inside the bell's echo. "Hsieh" is the Chinese word for shoe – and that was the only part of Ko-ai that had been saved.

Such is the legend of the great bell of Peking. And if you do not believe it, then travel to the city yourself and wait for the bell to be struck. Then you will hear the scream followed by the whisper and if anybody asks you what the sound is, you will be able to tell them.

# THE MONKEY WHO WOULD BE KING
## CHINESE

The Chinese tell many stories about a monkey whose full name was Sun Hou-tzu and who was hatched from an egg at the top of a mountain on the eastern side of the ocean. Although he was only a monkey, a wizard taught Sun all the secrets of the art of magic and soon he was able to change into 72 different forms and could jump thirty-six thousand miles with a single bound.

Sun was not a villain to begin with. It was he who organized all the world's monkeys into a single great army. By putting them all on the same side, he made sure that there was nobody for them to fight against which is why the monkeys have always been at peace. Unfortunately, this accomplishment went to his head and he began to get rather too big for his boots.

Stealing a magic sword from the Dragon King of the Eastern Sea, he made a nuisance of himself in all sorts of different ways. He got drunk at a banquet and woke up in Hell, where he promptly killed the two devils who guarded him and tore his name out of the Book of the Dead. This meant he could never die. He was sent up to Heaven where he looked after the stables, but when he got bored with that, he broke down one of Heaven's walls and escaped back to Earth.

Soon all the gods and goddesses were furious with him. The entire army of Heaven set out after him and although he fought valiently, changing into all 72 of his different shapes, he was caught and sentenced to death. But because he couldn't die, it was decided instead to melt him down in the furnace of a famous wizard called Laozi.

Laozi made his furnace white hot and dropped the monkey inside, slamming the lid. Sun remained there for forty-nine days, but then, when nobody was looking, he opened the lid and sprang out. By that time he was white hot with anger. Snatching up his magic sword, he announced himself the King of Heaven and threatened to kill everyone who lived there.

Now the August Personage of Jade, who was the proper ruler of Heaven, was at his wits' end. He could not kill the monkey and it seemed he could not keep him a prisoner. So in despair he sent for the one being who was more powerful than him – more powerful, in fact, than anyone or anything in the universe. The Buddha.

And so the Buddha came and asked the monkey what all the fuss was about.

"I want to be King of Heaven," the monkey told him.

"Do you think you are ready for such a position?" the Buddha asked, with a gentle sigh.

"Of course I am," the monkey snapped. "I'm ready for anything. Did you know, for example, that I can change myself into seventy-two different shapes? And that I can jump thirty-six thousand miles with one bound? I bet you can't jump that far."

"You think yourself more powerful than me?" the Buddha asked.

"I most certainly do."

"Let us see, then, my little friend. Show me how far you can jump. But to prove that you really go as far as you say, write your name on the ground when you get there."

So the monkey took a deep breath, crouched down and with all his strength leapt into the air. It was a fantastic jump. He soared up into the sky, broke through the clouds and continued into outer space, past the planets, right out of the solar system and beyond the stars. At last he landed in the middle of a great desert where two huge trenches met in the ground in front of him. Nothing grew for thousands of miles in any direction, but he could see that the ground was laced with a network of lines, making intricate patterns as they crossed over one another. Sun Hou-tzu had no idea where he was, but he was terrifically pleased with himself. He signed his name on the ground with a great flourish and jumped all the way back again.

"Not bad," the Buddha said. "But I'm sure you can do even better than that. Why not try again? And this time put all your strength into it."

"All right," Sun said.

He puffed himself up so much that he looked more like a frog than a monkey. Then he scrunched himself into a ball and finally catapulted himself off the ground with legs like rockets. This time he shot through the universe so quickly that he was just a blur. Not only did he break out of the solar system, but he passed the five red pillars which mark the boundary of the created world. At last he landed, this time on the edge of a perfectly circular cliff. A white precipice jutted out just below the ground on which he stood and beneath that all was darkness. The height almost made him dizzy, but he still signed his name as he had been told before jumping all the way back.

"There you are!" he said to the Buddha, unable to stop himself sneering. "I have proved that I am more powerful even than you. Could you have jumped that far? Of course not! Only the monkey could do it!"

"Wretched creature!" the Buddha cried, getting angry for the first time. He stretched out his hand. "See here the full extent of your vanity. You have signed your name twice on my right hand. The first time you landed on my palm, between my life line and my line of destiny. The second time you reached as far as the tip of my index finger and stood above my nail. Look where you have made your mark. It is the evidence of your own limitations!"

Now the monkey was afraid and began to tremble. He opened his mouth to speak, but it was too late for words.

The Buddha seized the wretched creature and shut him up in a magic mountain. And there he remained until the day that he forgot his ambitions and realised that although a monkey can rule the world, only the Buddha is fit to rule the kingdom of Heaven.

# THE FIRST ECLIPSE
## JAPANESE

There have been good gods and there have been bad gods, but there have been few gods as difficult and as generally objectionable as Susanoo, the Japanese god of the sea, of thunder, rain and wind, and of fertility. Perhaps his early years were partly to blame. It cannot be very easy growing up in the knowledge that you started life in your father's nose. But then his sister, Amaterasu, sprang to life at the same moment from her father's left eye and she was as divine as only a goddess of the sun can be.

But to begin at the beginning . . .

The father of Susanoo and Amaterasu was called Izanagi. He was one of the first of the Japanese gods and the father of virtually all the gods that followed – as well as of the eight principle islands of Japan. His marriage came to a tragic end, however, when his wife, whose name was Izanami, was burned to death while giving birth to the god of fire. Izanagi wept bitterly at her loss and more gods sprang from his every tear. In his anger, he cut the head off the god of fire and yet more gods were born in the splashing of blood. All this goes some way towards explaining why there are so many gods in Japan.

Meanwhile, Izanami had gone down to the Underworld and Izanagi decided to carry her back.

"Am I not a god?" he said to himself. "Am I not the father of all the gods? Why should she be taken from me?

Izanami is beautiful. Her skin is so fair, her hair so dark, her eyes so like the colour of emeralds. I will not live without her! She shall come back to me."

And with these words he hurried down to the Underworld and banged on the door of the house in which she was living.

"Izanami!" he called out. "It is me. Izanagi. I have come to take you home."

"Leave me!" a voice cried from within. "I am not ready for you. Go and speak with the king of the Underworld. He will tell you when I can leave."

"Nobody tells me anything!" Izanagi shouted, growing angry. "I am the god of the gods and you will come with me."

"Not yet!"

"You will come this instant."

Now red with anger, Izanagi kicked down the door and walked into the house. But he had forgotten the destructive power of death. The sight that greeted him on the other side of the door was not his beautiful wife but a hideous spectacle, a rotting, decomposing corpse with worms where there should have been eyes, glistening bones where there should have been soft flesh. With a terrible scream he turned and ran. He did not stop running until he had left the Underworld and reached the sea. Without even stopping to take a breath, he dived in. At once the sound of his own screams was cut off, and his body turned slowly in a world of shimmering blue silence, his robes billowing around him and bubbles streaming from his nose and mouth. It was as if he needed the expanse of a whole ocean to cleanse the horror of what he had seen. And so it was. The icy water shattered the memory, then washed away the fragments. When he climbed onto the shore, Izanami and her home in the Underworld were forgotten.

Susanoo and Amaterasu were born at the same moment beneath the ocean, carried away from their father's body in a whirlpool of bubbles. When at last they reached the surface, their father was already gone, turning his back on them. And so it was that the god of the sea and the goddess of the sun were born.

### Susanoo Goes Too Far

While Amaterasu quietly took her place in the heavens, providing the world with light and warmth, Susanoo — whose name can be translated to mean "swift, headstrong god" — took every opportunity to squabble with his father. At last the old god came to the end of his tether and after a particularly violent disagreement, banished his son to the province of Izumo which is on the coast of the Sea of Japan.

Before he went, however, he decided to travel up to heaven in order to say goodbye to his sister, whom he had not seen since they were born. As usual he went with a great deal of noise and confusion, shaking the mountains and making the whole world tremble. Hearing him coming, Amaterasu grew alarmed. A stampede of elephants or an army on the warpath would have made less of a commotion. Certainly it was not the sound of a brother coming to visit. Afraid for her life, she reached for her bow and when Susanoo arrived, he found the point of an arrow aimed straight at his heart.

"Keep back!" Amaterasu warned.

"What the . . . what the blazes!" Susanoo cried. "Our honourable father kicks me out of the heavens and now my beloved sister wants to pin me to a cloud!"

"Why have you come?"

"To say goodbye."

"Goodbye?" Still she aimed the arrow at her brother, the bowstring taut in her fingers. "Why should I believe you?"

"Because I'm your brother, for heaven's sake! Look – I'll tell you what. Let us, you and I, create eight more gods. They'll be a sort of token between us, proof that no matter what may happen now or in the future, we remain brother and sister, and friends. Our children will be the founders of the royal house of Japan and everyone will know that we were their parents. Our children! What do you say?"

Then Amaterasu's heart softened. She set down her bow and arrow and took instead her brother's sword which she broke into three pieces. These she placed in her mouth. A moment later she blew out a silvery mist in which three young girls appeared. For his part, Susanoo reached for the five jewels that hung on his sister's necklace and broke them between his teeth. Five young gods leapt out of the pieces. Five boys and three girls: thus were the first ancestors of the Japanese created.

Amaterasu smiled to see what she had done. But as usual,

Susanoo's excitement was so great as to be positively dangerous. First he ruined all the rice-fields by filling in the irrigation ditches. Then he caused havoc in the sacred temple that had been built for the fruit festival. Finally he ran, laughing, up to his elderly horse and − rather in the manner of a conjuror whipping away a tablecloth without disturbing the cups and plates − pulled off the wretched animal's skin in one piece. The bloody corpse he hurled into the air and, still shrieking with laughter, hurried off to find something else to destroy.

All this was bad enough but what was even worse was that the horse landed on the roof of Amaterasu's house, smashing right through in a shower of tiles and straw. It finally came to rest in the sewing room.

Amaterasu was sewing at the time.

You can imagine how she felt. There she was one minute putting a final stitch in the hem of a kimono. The next, the roof was collapsing all around her and a great lump of dead horse was splattering itself all over her sewing-machine. In a second the whole room was a mass of screaming women. Two servants fainted. A third fell into her machine and managed to stitch a perfect line across her own throat before she succumbed. As for Amaterasu, she was so frightened that she ran out of the house and hid herself in a dark cave, pulling an enormous boulder across the entrance so that no one could follow her in. At once the world was plunged into darkness.

And that, some scholars say, was the first eclipse.

## The Rival

Susanoo received a severe punishment for his misbehaviour. He had already been banished from heaven, but now his beard and moustache were cut off and all his fingernails and toenails were pulled out with tweezers. As a matter of fact, he became something of a reformed character after this, performing many great and heroic deeds in the province of Izumo.

But meanwhile, the other gods were faced with a problem. They had seen Amaterasu run into the cave, so at least they knew where to find her. The question was, how could they entice her out and so end the darkness that had fallen on the world? One god suggested brute force, but that was soon rejected, as Amaterasu would only hide again once they had gone. Another suggested bribing her with a nice juicy snake, but after her experience with the flayed horse, nobody believed this would work. At last a god who was known as "Treasure-thoughts" came up with an idea.

Hundreds of the gods set to work at once. There was a simple Sakaki tree growing on a hillside outside the cave and they decorated its branches with fabulous jewels, brightly coloured ribbons and tiny mirrors. Then they began to sing, to dance and to play musical instruments usually only brought out for the most important religious celebrations.

Hearing the noise, Amaterasu rolled back the stone and poked her head out. The sight that greeted her eyes astonished her. There were no fewer than eight hundred gods dancing outside the cave. Some were dressed only in bamboo leaves; others had stripped off altogether, much to the delight of the remainder who were howling with laughter and stamping their feet.

"What's happening?" Amaterasu demanded.

One of the gods turned and smiled at her. "Oh hello, Amaterasu," he said. "We thought you'd locked yourself away for ever."

"So why are you celebrating?"

"Because now we've got a goddess who's even more beautiful than you. She's going to take over."

"More beautiful than me?" Amaterasu's eyes opened wide. "And where can I find this . . . goddess?"

"She's just over there."

Amaterasu took three steps out of the cave. And there, a short distance away, she saw her rival. The "goddess" was sparkling brilliantly, living flames of colour erupting from a cataclysm of blinding white. Ribbons of colour fluttered in the breeze around her. Amaterasu took another three steps forwards. The colours grew even more dazzling, even more divine.

What she did not realise was that she was seeing only her own reflection, captured by the mirrors and the jewels on the Sakaki tree. For as she left the cave, her own golden light was returning to the heavens, bringing with it her own warmth, colour and life. When she was nine steps away, the god of Force suddenly leapt down and rolled the boulder back into place, tying it down so that the entrance was sealed. Then Amaterasu realised that she had been tricked.

But she was more angry with herself for being jealous of her own reflection than she was with the other gods for their cunning. And so she agreed to return to her place in the heavens. And that was the end of the first eclipse.

# THE FABULOUS SPOTTED EGG
## CHEYENNE INDIAN

The Cheyenne Indians, who rode the plains of North America in the seventeenth and eighteenth centuries, had a strange custom. Whenever they came to a wide stretch of water — a lake or a river, perhaps — they would throw some food or tobacco in before they rode across. Nobody asked the Cheyennes why they did this, but then, of course, nobody asked the Cheyennes anything. If you met a Cheyenne, it was safer just to run away.

Well, there was a reason. It was contained in a tale told by the Cheyenne storytellers, a tale about a great river monster and two brothers who discovered a fabulous spotted egg.

The two brothers — their names aren't known, but we'll call them Elder and Younger — had managed to get themselves lost on the prairie. The horizon made a great big circle all around them and there was nothing to see except the grass, waving in the wind. The brothers had a little water, but they had no food.

They walked a few miles and they got hungrier and hungrier, and soon the rumble of their stomachs was accompanying the rustle of the wind. Then all of a sudden they came upon an egg just lying on the ground with no sign of a bird or a nest anywhere near.

"Well, that's a stroke of luck," Younger said. "Look at that egg. I reckon it'll last the two of us a whole week."

"I'm not so sure," Elder growled. "It doesn't look too healthy to me."

"What do you mean?" Younger cried. "It's just an egg."

But if it was just an egg, it was just a very peculiar egg. For a start, it was bright green with red spots. Also it was enormous – much bigger than a chicken egg. Much bigger, in fact, than a chicken. And how had it got there? It was, after all, in the middle of the prairie.

"It looks magic to me," Elder said. "I say we don't touch it."

"Come on!" Younger replied. "It was probably laid by a bird or a turtle or something. Okay, so it's a funny colour. But I'm so hungry, I'd eat a green and red spotted horse!"

So while Elder watched, Younger lit a bonfire and roasted the egg. Then he cracked the shell and began to eat.

"You sure you don't want some?" he asked.

"No, thanks," Elder said.

"It's really good. You don't know what you're missing."

In fact, Younger was lying when he said that. The egg was hard and rubbery. The yolk was green, the same colour as the shell, and the white wasn't white but a sort of pink. And it didn't taste like an egg should. It tasted of fish.

Now even as Younger ate he began to feel sick, but something made him go on eating. He couldn't stop. Faster and faster he spooned the egg down until it had all gone and only the shell was left.

"I hope you know what you're doing," Elder muttered.

The next morning, when they woke up, Younger was feeling really ill. His stomach was like a funfair merry-go-round and his eyes were as big as ping-pong balls. Worst of all, he was really thirsty. He drank all the water in his bottle but it could have been a thimblefull for all the good it did him. Elder looked at him and sighed.

"You look terrible," he said.

"I feel terrible," Younger agreed.

"You're green!"

"Green?"

"And you've got red spots."

Younger stood up. "Let's go!" he said. "The sooner we find water, the better. I need a drink."

They walked until sunset, by which time Younger's skin had gone greener and his spots had got redder. Also all his hair had fallen out and he seemed to be having trouble talking.

"Sssssay," he hissed. "Do you reckon I made a misssssstake eating that egg?"

"I guess so, kid," Elder replied.

"I guesssss it was kind of sssssstupid. But I'll feel better when I get to water. I really want a sssssswim."

The next morning he was worse. His arms had somehow glued themselves to his sides and his nose had dropped off. He was a vivid green and red and his skin was slimy. Like a snake's.

"I feel worsssssse," he moaned.

"You look worse," Elder said.

"Water!"

They reached water at sunset.

Younger, whose legs had almost melted into one

another, decided that he would rather sleep in the river while Elder curled up on land beside a bonfire. Elder hadn't eaten for five days now and he was weak and tired. It didn't take him long to fall asleep.

He was woken up by the sound of singing. He opened his eyes and the first thing he saw was a great heap of fish lying on the bank, waiting to be cooked. Then he looked beyond, in the water, and saw his brother.

Except that it wasn't really his brother any more. The boy had become an enormous sea-monster with huge teeth, scales and a forked tail. He was swimming to and fro, stopping now and then to fork another fish with the point of his tail and flip it onto the bank.

"Hey, kid!" Elder called out. "How are you feeling today?"

"Fine!" Younger replied. "It'sssss not ssssso bad being a ssssssea-sssssserpent. And I've caught a whole lot of fisssssh!"

"Thanks!" Elder said.

"Hey – lisssssten," Younger continued. "Don't you forget about me. I got you food, ssssso you get me food. I don't want to eat fissssssh all my life."

"I'll do that," Elder promised.

"And tobacco too. Just because I'm a monssssssster, it doesn't mean I can't sssssssmoke!"

And that is why the Cheyennes always stopped and threw food or tobacco into the water before they crossed it (even when they were being chased by the cavalry). It was to keep the sea-serpent singing.

# GERIGUIAGUIATUGO
## BORORO INDIAN

The Bororo Indians of South America tell a strange story about a young man with the difficult name of Geriguiaguiatugo. There are many versions of the story (for the Indians never wrote it down), but it usually begins with Geriguiaguiatugo violently attacking his mother in the forest. Quite what the poor woman had done to deserve this battering isn't known, but that's how the story starts.

Anyway, with his mother lying in the local witch-doctor's hut, Geriguiaguiatugo returned to his village and went on living as if nothing had happened. His father, however, was suspicious. It was nothing he could put his finger on — the bruises on his son's knuckles or the enormous bloodstains on his shirt, perhaps — but he somehow felt certain that the boy was responsible for his wife's terrible injuries.

To get his revenge, therefore, he sent him on a number of perilous missions, each one more dangerous than the last. For example, he ordered him to remove a sacred rattle from the Lake of Souls. This lake was a dreadful place where dead men's hands would break through the black surface of the water to drag unsuspecting travellers down to a freezing death. But Geriguiaguiatugo survived. Guided by a humming-bird, he sailed right across, snatched the sacred rattle and brought it back to the village whistling so cheerfully that you might have thought he'd just popped down to the newsagent for a pound of jelly babies.

His father tried again – and this time he came with him. They were going in search of a rare parrot, he explained, and one that could only be found at the top of a cliff some distance from the village. The cliff, when they reached it, however, was fantastically high. Standing at the bottom with his neck bent back, Geriguiaguiatugo could not see where the sheer rock face ended and the sky began. It seemed to go on forever.

"How will we ever get to the top?" he asked.

His father drove an iron nail into the cliff-face, missing his son's head by inches. "We'll climb," he said.

And so they did. It was slow, gruelling work. There were hardly any footholds and what few ledges or outcrops they could find were tiny and treacherous. One moment your foot would be firmly fixed against the cliff. The next, your stomach would lurch and you would scrabble madly for support while the crumbling rocks and pebbles that were until a moment ago beneath your foot tumbled to the ground below. And soon the ground was far, far below. Looking down, Geriguiaguiatugo could see trees that were now no bigger than daisies. But generally he preferred not to look down. Swearing under his breath, he concentrated on searching for a way to conquer the next six inches of the cliff.

His father was climbing directly beneath him. At one stage even the merest hint of a foothold disappeared and Geriguiaguiatugo had to hammer in a whole staircase of nails that stretched for about thirty feet. That was when his father struck. Using his bare hands, he pulled out all the nails, cut the rope that separated him from his son, and climbed back down the way he had come. When he turned round, Geriguiaguiatugo found himself either half-way up or half-way down the cliff but certainly going nowhere.

"You filthy rotter!" he shouted. "You can't leave me here!"

"Yes I can!" came back the cheery reply.

"Come back! What about the mission? What about the blooming parrot? What about me?"

But his father just laughed.

Soon he had disappeared out of sight all together and Geriguiaguiatugo was forced to take stock of his situation. It was not a pleasant one. His hands were raw and bleeding after all his effort. Night was drawing in. Although he still had the hammer and the bag of nails, it was physically impossible to knock in a fresh staircase underneath his feet. And yet without the staircase, there was certainly no way down. The cliff-face was too smooth, too dangerous.

That just left up.

He began to climb. He climbed until every muscle in his body screamed at him and tears ran down his cheeks.

"What'd I do to deserve this?" he moaned, (forgetting, for the moment, his hospitalised mother). "It's not fair. Rare parrots? I'll rare parrot him . . . "

One slip and the story would have ended then and there, but somehow Geriguiaguiatugo managed to reach the top. His troubles, however, were far from over. As his father had known from the very start, there was nothing there. No plants, no water, no birds . . . not so much as a rare parrot's feather. He had reached the top but it seemed that all that awaited him was a slow death by starvation.

By now the sun had gone down and a pale moon hung in the sky. But after his life in the jungle, Geriguiaguiatugo could see as well by night as by day and he was surprised to discover that he was no longer alone. A whole colony of lizards inhabited the arid rocks at the top of the cliff and now that the heat of the day was over, they were coming out to stretch themselves in the dust. Now, among the Bororo Indians, lizard is something of a delicacy. It comes at its best sautéed in a little butter and flavoured with herbs. But it's just as good crunched raw between the teeth. In a matter of seconds, Geriguiaguiatugo had caught a couple of dozen fat specimens, stunning them with his hammer. Five he ate. The rest he hung on a string around his belt.

The next day, when he woke up, the sun was hotter than ever. It was far too hot even to think about finding a way off the cliff, so Geriguiaguiatugo just sat there, amusing himself by dreaming up ever more fiendish things to do to his father when − or if − he got back to the village. Around midday, he began to notice an unpleasant smell. By one o'clock it was a horrible smell. He got up and walked over to the other side of the cliff-top. The smell followed him. An hour later it had become so bad that he reeled, staggered, then fainted dead away.

The dead lizards were to blame. Hanging around his waist in the hot sun, the corpses had all gone off – and now their stench attracted a passing flock of vultures. The ghastly birds with their bald heads, ragged green feathers and twisting necks liked their meat best when it was well hung. As one they landed on the unconscious body of Geriguiaguiatugo and began to tear into the rotten flesh with their teeth and talons. And so hungry were they, they didn't stop with the lizards. Although they probably didn't notice it, they also managed to eat both of Geriguiaguiatugo's buttocks. His buttocks and the dead lizards probably tasted much the same.

Geriguiaguiatugo woke up some time later and he was so relieved to find that the smell had gone that he didn't even notice that he no longer had a bottom. A short distance away, the vultures watched as he explored the edge of the cliff, searching for a way down. After such a delicious meal, the ugly birds were kindly disposed towards the Indian, particularly as they had just disposed of a large part of his person.

"Let's take him to the bottom," one suggested.

"You mean . . . his bottom?" another asked.

"No! No! The bottom of the cliff."

"If we leave him here, he's got precious little future ahead of him," a third remarked.

"He's got precious little behind him too," a fourth observed.

So the birds flew back to Geriguiaguiatugo and, hooking

their claws into his shirt, lifted him clear off the ground and carried him all the way to the foot of the cliff.

"My dear birdies," the astonished Indian said, "I thank you. Really I do. From the bottom of my heart."

"And from the heart of your bottom," sniggered one of the vultures.

As soon as they had gone, Geriguiaguiatugo began the journey back to the village, pausing only to pluck some fruit from a tree, for he was hungry again. It was then that he discovered what had happened to him. For, having no bottom, the fruit literally went straight through him. But he wasn't put out. He remembered how his grandmother had used to make him eat his mashed potato when he was a little boy – forming it into shapes on his plate. How he had loved that old lady! He had only put her into hospital half a dozen times and she had never needed more than fifteen stitches. Now, remembering her wisdom, he dug up some sweet potatoes, boiled and mashed them and finally formed them into a new pair of buttocks which he fitted neatly into place.

Thus equipped, he made his way back to his village. The journey took him several weeks but even so, the villagers were still celebrating his supposed death when he got back. Although they immediately tried to pretend that they were actually mourning for him, Geriguiaguiatugo wasn't fooled. Nor was he impressed when his father crawled forward to greet him.

"Hello, son," his father said, trying to fix a smile to his

lips even as the blood drained from his face.

"Hello, Dad," Geriguiaguiatugo replied. "Been doing any rock climbing lately?"

"Well . . . er . . . you see . . . I did try to get back to you. Honest! But . . . "

"But?"

"But . . . "

"I'll butt you, you old buffoon!"

And with those words, Geriguiaguiatugo magically transformed himself into a stag and charged at his father, butting him to the ground. The villagers groaned, but he wasn't finished yet. He hooked his horns into his father's shirt and then shot the old man into the air with one flick of his neck. Three times he did it. The first time, his father landed in a clump of thistles. The second time he hit a wasp's nest. And the third time he splashed into a nearby river, where he was immediately torn into a million pieces by a pack of ravenous piranha fish.

After that, Geriguiaguiatugo ruled over the village. And you can be sure that they all lived horribly ever after.

# THE TEN FINGERS OF SEDNA
### ESKIMO

The gods and goddesses of the Eskimos are more to be feared than admired, for, like the wind that howls across the Bering Straits and the snow that slices down on Hudson Bay, they are savage and without pity. The most feared of all of them is Sedna. Sedna the sea-goddess. Sedna the giant. Sedna with her bedraggled hair and gaping socket where one eye has been torn out.

Once Sedna was a beautiful young Eskimo girl, the only daughter of a widowed father. So beautiful was she that as she grew up, a great many young men came from near and far in the hope of marrying her. But Sedna was a vain, haughty girl, too well-aware of her own good looks. She enjoyed teasing the young men, leading them on one minute, rejecting them the next. Sometimes she would whisper tales or choose a favourite, just for the pleasure of seeing them fight over her. And they did fight. Men killed for the love of Sedna, but she still refused to marry.

Then one day a man arrived at the village, a man much handsomer than any who had come before. The kayak he came in was decorated with jewels and more jewels glittered in the necklace that hung across his breast. He wore the finest furs and carried a spear of pure white ivory. The young man didn't even get out of his canoe. Instead, he called out to Sedna.

"Come with me, Sedna! Come and be my wife!"

"Why?" Sedna called back. "What can you give me?"

"You shall live in my house on the edge of a cliff," the young man cried. "You will never be hungry, for I will bring you meat every day. You will sleep on a bearskin with a blanket of feathers and you will never have to work."

To Sedna, this sounded almost too good to be true. And the young man was very handsome. Without another thought, she packed her bags and got into the kayak, never to be seen by the villagers again.

The boat sailed away. For two days and two nights they sailed and the further they went, the more the young man seemed to change. First his ivory spear and jewels disappeared. Then his skins fell away to reveal a sort of undershirt of feathers. His eyes grew beady and the feathers spread across his face. But it was only when they arrived at his home that the spell was finally broken. For the man was not a man at all but a bird-spirit with the power to take on human form. Flying above the village he had seen Sedna and had determined to make her his wife – even if he had to use magic and trickery to do it.

So Sedna began life married to a bird. The house on the edge of the cliff turned out to be a nest perched on a rocky crag. The meat that the bird had promised her was nothing more than freshly killed gulls and kittiwakes. The blanket of feathers was the bird's own wing, and although it was true that she never had to work, nor was she able to do anything except groan and cry and bitterly curse the day that she had left the village.

The story might have ended there had her father not grown more and more lonely without her. She had never been a perfect daughter, it was true, but when you have only one daughter and your wife is dead, you are ready to overlook temper tantrums and whining and general ungratefulness. So he set out to search for her and after a great many weeks he found her still sitting in the nest bemoaning her fate.

By a stroke of luck, the bird-spirit was away, searching for food for his wife – she had demanded something a bit more delicate than freshly killed kittiwake – so she was able to tell her father what had happened.

"He's not a man, he's a bird!" she wailed. "And I want to go home!"

"My poor child . . . " the father began.

"Don't you 'poor child' me!" Sedna cried. "If you'd only looked after me a little better, this would never have happened. Now let's get moving. He'll be back any minute."

The father helped his daughter climb down the cliff. They reached the bottom and ran across the beach to where his kayak was anchored. Sedna didn't want to get her feet wet and her father had to lift her into the boat and that wasted a bit of time, but soon they were sailing away, leaving the nest far behind them.

But then the bird-spirit returned. It saw the empty nest, the footprints in the sand and the boat, already just a speck on the horizon, and let out a great cry. For in its own way it had loved Sedna. It alone had been blind to her faults and it really had tried to make her happy in the nest.

Now it soared after them, its great white wings carrying it swiftly across the sea. In minutes it had reached the boat, hovering in the air above it, its eyes filled with tears.

"Come back, Sedna!" it cried. "You are my wife. I need you!"

"Go away!" Sedna replied. "Do you really think I'm going to spend my life married to a bird? Leave me alone!"

"Please . . . "

The bird-spirit swooped down as if to perch on the edge of the boat and at that moment the father swung his oar. The wood crashed into the bird-spirit, knocking it over backwards. The poor creature almost plunged into the sea, but then it recovered and, realising that it had lost Sedna forever, flew away, crying softly.

The bird-spirit had no sooner disappeared than the weather changed. The surface of the sea had been still and flat but now an Arctic storm sprang up. The waves rose and fell. Icy-cold water pounded against the boat, spinning it out of control. The father struggled with the oars but it was useless. The spray blinded him. The wind tore at his clothes. Black clouds had smothered the sky and now forks of lightning crackled down all around them.

"Do something!" Sedna cried. "Don't just sit there . . . !"

"It's your fault!" her father exclaimed in a hoarse voice. "The sea is angry because you've left your husband."

There was a deafening crash of thunder. A wave as high as a mountain rose up beside them, almost turning the boat upside-down.

"We're going to die!" Sedna wept. "Why didn't you just leave me where I was? If you hadn't come for me, this would never have happened. If you . . . "

But then she stopped because a mad look had come into her father's eyes. Somehow he stood up in the rocking boat and grabbed hold of her.

"What are you doing?" she demanded.

"It's your fault," her father rasped. "And perhaps if I throw you overboard . . . yes . . . if I throw you overboard, then the sea will forgive me, then everything will be all right."

"You're mad! Leave me alone!"

"You must die, Sedna. I should never have come for you."

As the boat heaved up and down and whirled round in circles, as the lightning flashed and the thunder roared, the two of them fought in the tiny boat. At one point it seemed that Sedna might win, for she was the taller and the stronger of the two, but then somehow her father's thumb found her eye. There was another crash of thunder. Blood poured down her cheek. She staggered backwards and fell overboard.

But still she clung onto the edge of the boat, desperately trying to pull herself back in. With an insane laugh, the father seized his ivory axe. With the wind racing around him, he held it high above his head, then brought it hurtling down. It severed five of Sedna's fingers.

Sedna screamed.

The fingers fell into the foaming sea and turned into seals.

The father struck again with the axe.

Sedna screamed a second time.

The five fingers of her other hand fell into the water and became whales. Sedna disappeared beneath the surface.

The storm died down and the sea grew calm. Unable to go any further, the father turned the boat in towards the shore and pitched his tent on a rocky outcrop on the edge of the beach. He knew that he had done wrong but he was too exhausted and too glad to be alive. Almost at once he fell into a deep sleep.

That night there was an unusually high tide. The water came in further than it had ever done before, further than it has ever done since. It came in so far, in fact, that the old man drowned in his sleep. And as the waves lapped over one another, you could almost imagine that the sound they made was the sound of laughter.

# GIVEN TO THE SUN
## INCA

"Why do we Incas worship the Sun?" the boy asked.

"Have you not been taught that at school?" the Inca priest demanded crossly.

"I am too young to have gone to school," the boy replied.

The priest softened. "Very well," he said. "I will tell you the story of how the Sun came into the land . . . "

"There was a time, long, long ago, when the whole land was covered in darkness, when there was nothing but rocky mountains and plunging cliffs. The people knew nothing then. They lived like animals, going naked in the fields, without shame. They had neither houses nor villages but lived in caves, huddling together for warmth, unable even to light a fire. They fed on wild fruit and whatever animals they could catch, tearing at the meat with their teeth and swallowing it raw. When times were hard, they ate grass or the roots of weeds and wild plants and sometimes (horrible to say) they might even feast on human flesh.

"Then came Inti — for that is the name we have given to the Sun, a name that only a true Inca may utter — and his light lit the world and showed up the wretched state of the people. And because the Sun was kind, he was ashamed for them. So he decided to send one of his sons down from heaven to earth. It would be his job to show men and women how to till the soil, how to sow seed, to raise cattle, to bring in the fruits of the harvest. He would also teach men and women to worship the Sun as their god, for without light and warmth they could be no better than animals."

"What was the name of the son of the Sun?" the boy asked.

"His name was Manco Capac," the priest said. "And with him came Occlo Huaco. She was the daughter of the Moon."

"Was the Sun the friend of the Moon?"

"They were married to each other," the priest explained. "So the two children were brother and sister."

"The son and daughter of the Sun were set down on two islands in Lake Titicaca, which is the highest lake in the world. Even to this day they are known as the Islands of the Sun and the Moon. Then they walked across the lake, the water sparkling like diamonds at their feet, until at last they stepped onto dry land and began their work.

"Before they had left heaven, the Sun had given them a rod of gold. It was about as thick as two fingers and a little shorter than a man's arm.

"'Go where you will,' (he had told them), 'but whenever you stop to sleep or to eat, try pushing this rod into the earth. If it won't go in, or only goes in a little way, keep moving. But when you reach a spot where, with a single thrust, the rod disappears completely, you will know that you are in a place that is sacred to me. And there you must stay. It will become the site for a great city, full of palaces and temples. And that city will be the centre of my empire, an empire such as has never been seen before in the world.'

"Manco Capac and Occlo Huaco left Lake Titicaca and began walking towards the north. Every day, they tried to push their rod of gold into the earth, but without success. This went on for many weeks, until at last they came to the valley of Cuzco which was then nothing more than a wild, mountainous desert. When they tried their rod here, it disappeared completely into the ground so they knew they had reached the place where the Inca empire was to be founded.

"The two of them then went their own ways, talking to the savages they met and explaining why they had come. The savages, of course, were hugely impressed. For the strangers were dressed in beautiful clothes. Gold discs hung from their ears. Their hair was short and tidy and their bodies were clean. There had never been two people like them, and soon thousands of men and women had come to the valley of Cuzco to see them and to hear what they had to say.

"Then it was that Manco Capac began building the city that his father had demanded. At the same time, he and his sister taught the people everything they needed to know if they were to be properly civilized."

"Was the city the same city that we are in now?" the boy asked.

"Yes," the priest said. "It was called Cuzco. And it was divided into two halves. Upper Cuzco was built by our king. Lower Cuzco was built by the queen."

"Why were there two halves?"

"It was built like the human body, with a right side and a left side. All our cities have been built the same way. But the Sun is rising, boy. We must make an end soon . . ."

"In only a short time, the savages were savage no more. They lived in brick houses and wore proper clothing. Manco Capac had taught the men how to cultivate the fields while his sister had taught the women how to spin and weave. There was even an army in Cuzco with bows and arrows and spears, ready to fight those people who still remained in the wild. But gradually the empire spread and Manco Capac became the first Inca, which is to say the first king of the Inca people.

"Always since then, the Incas have worshipped the Sun. For every Inca king who reigns is a descendant of Manco Capac and so a descendant of the Sun. The Sun gives light and warmth and makes the crops grow. The Sun sent his own son into the world so that the people would no longer behave like animals. Great temples have been built to honour the Sun, reflecting his rays in sheets of beaten gold.

"And on Inti Raymi – which is the summer solstice, the day when the Sun is at the furthest extreme of his journey south – then there is a festival with music and dancing and feasting. On that day, sacrifices are made. Llamas have their throats cut and then they are burnt. The smoke rises into the air and in this way they are given to the Sun. And if there is a special event to be celebrated, a great victory for example, then it is not an animal but a child who must die."

"And I am to be given to the Sun," the boy whispered.

"That is your honour, boy," the priest said.

The Sun had risen above the horizon now. The priest forced the boy back against the sacrificial stone, then thrust the ceremonial knife deep into his heart. A fire was lit. And soon the smoke was curling upwards, up into the brilliant sky.

# CATCHING THE SUN
## POLYNESIAN

To look at, you would not have thought that Maui was a hero. He was very small and very ugly with short, stubby arms and a pot belly. It will come as no surprise to learn that the moment he was born — the fifth of five brothers — his mother picked him up and hurled him into the sea. And yet to the Polynesian people, Maui was one of the greatest if not the greatest of the so-called trickster heroes — which is to say that what he lacked in dignity and grace he made up for in cunning.

He was saved from drowning by his ancestor-in-the-sky, a god called Tama-hui-ki-te-rangi and, dripping wet, with a piece of seaweed dangling behind one ear, made his way to the House of Assembly, where his brothers had just been christened. There was a party going on when he arrived, as there is at every Polynesian christening. All the family had been invited and the various relatives were eating their way through baskets piled high with seafood and fruit, drinking exotic cocktails and dancing together under the stars.

This festive atmosphere was abruptly shattered by the appearance of the small and dripping hero.

"Who are you?" his mother demanded.

"I am your son," Maui replied, rather grumpily.

"Impossible!" the mother sniffed. "I threw you away the moment you were born."

"Well, I've come back," Maui retorted. "And I'd be

grateful if you would be so good as to christen me instead of trying to throw me away again."

Then Maui's father stepped forward.

"How do we know you are who you say you are?" he asked. "You don't look like your brothers. You could be anybody's child."

Maui smiled.

"I can prove it," he said, walking over to where his four brothers were sitting, gurgling like ordinary babies should. "This one is called Maui-taha," he continued, pointing. "This one is Maui-roto. He's Maui-poe. And he's Maui-waho."

His mother's jaw dropped. "How do you know?" she asked.

"I spent nine months in the same womb as them," Maui snapped. "I ought to have got to know their names!"

When they heard this, his parents were forced to accept that he was their lost son. His father plucked the seaweed off his ear and gave him a towel. His mother apologised for throwing him into the sea. And with the simple name of Maui, he was welcomed into the family.

During the next few years, Maui had many adventures. Another ancestor of his – an ancestress, in fact, called Muri-ranga-whenua – gave him a magic jawbone and he never went anywhere without it. It was by using the magic jawbone that he was able to fish the land of New Zealand out of the sea, although once he had brought it to the surface, his brothers insisted on cutting it up. Naturally they made a botch job of it, and that is why there are so many mountains in New Zealand and so many irregularly shaped islands around it.

Maui's other feats included inventing the kite, the eel-pot and the barbed fishing spears still used by Polynesians to this day. He also single-handedly separated the earth and the sky (which were stuck together at the time), heaving the sky up rather like an Olympic athlete with a dumb-bell. But perhaps his most extraordinary feat, and the subject of this myth, was the catching of the sun.

The adventure began one evening, just as the sun was setting. He and his brothers had been out fishing but now, as the darkness set in, they were forced to return home. In those days, of course, there was no electricity or gas. The day ended in every sense of the word once it got dark.

"If only the sun stayed up longer," Maui said, "we'd all be better off."

The words were no sooner out of his mouth than he was struck by a thought.

"Hey!" he cried. "Why don't we catch it?"

His brothers looked at him wearily.

"We couldn't," one said. "It's too far away."

"And too big," added a second.

"And even if we did catch it," a third muttered, "it would only burn us up."

"It's impossible," the fourth agreed.

"Nonsense!" Maui shouted. "You're talking to the man who netted New Zealand and lifted up the sky. Of course we can do it!"

For the next week, the five brothers worked, spinning and twisting ropes to form the noose with which they would catch the sun. The technique they used to make the rope – plaiting the flax into stout, square-shaped lengths – was another invention which you will still find used in Polynesia. It is called tua-maka.

At last, when the rope was ready, they set off. They travelled only at night so that the sun, hidden beneath the horizon, would not see them coming. By day they hid in the desert, sleeping under bushes or covering themselves with a layer of sand. For several months they travelled, and in this way they finally arrived at the very eastern edge of the world.

Here, working under Maui's supervision, they built an enormous clay wall with two sheds – one at each end. The sheds were for the four brothers to hide in so that they would not get burnt by the sun. The noose was unpacked and dangled over the wall so that it hung in outer space – just underneath the world itself. Maui took his place, standing at the very centre of the world.

And thus prepared, they waited.

Dawn arrived and the unsuspecting sun began its climb.

"It's coming," Maui whispered, the light dancing in his eyes.

The brothers, hidden in their sheds, tightened their grips on the ends of the ropes.

The sun drew level with the wall.

"Now!" Maui cried, and slipped the noose over it.

At once the sun tried to back away. Brilliant flames exploded around it, tearing at the dark blue fabric of the universe. Burning meteors cascaded down in apocalyptic fury. Had Maui been an ordinary human, he would have been frazzled. But as the furious heat of the sun raced through him, he just laughed and pulled at the rope.

The noose tightened. The sun was caught.

"Now I'll teach you, you old rascal!" Maui giggled.

And, lifting his magic jawbone, he walloped the sun half a dozen times.

"Aaagh!" screamed the sun.

"Hold on!" Maui shouted at his brothers, for the ropes were jerking up and down like a snake stew. Again and again he pounded the sun with the jawbone, sparks flying every time it made contact.

"Stop it!" the sun yelled. "What have I done to you?"

But Maui was beside himself with excitement and didn't listen.

At last he tired of the sport. Climbing back down from the wall, he signalled his brothers, who allowed the noose to open again. The sun slipped out and continued its upwards climb.

But it was not the same sun that had once circled the earth in seven-and-a-half hours. Now it was bruised, battered and bewildered, quite exhausted by the clobbering it had received at Maui's hands. From that day on, it took twenty-four hours to make the round trip – twelve hours from horizon to horizon.

For Maui had not only caught the sun. He'd beaten the living daylight out of it too.

# DEATH AND THE BOY
## WEST AFRICAN

West Africa was gripped by the unrelenting hand of famine. Its arid breath whispered over the land, blighting the crops and blistering the livestock. Its shadow fell across the villages, stretching ever further in the remorseless sunlight. The water holes shrivelled and dried up. The mud hardened then cracked. Wherever the people went, black flies followed, sucking the last drops of moisture from the corners of their eyes and mouths. If famine was the king, the flies were its most loyal knights.

It was a cruel time. Every minute of every day became an exhausting struggle to find food, to break into the unyielding earth for water, to save the pathetically withered things that had been root vegetables or plants. The people struggled and prayed for rain. They knew they would survive. They had been through it all before.

But in one village there was a young boy who could work no longer. He had not eaten meat for so long (he thought) that he had forgotten what it tasted like. He was tired of the daily labouring, tired of seeing the blank determination that hung on the faces of his friends and relatives. And so one day he left the village, slipping away into the jungle to find his fortune – or at the very least, to renew his acquaintance with the flavour of meat.

For three days he walked without stumbling on so much as a parrot that he might pop into a pot. But on the third day, just as he was about to turn round and go home again, he came across something very peculiar. There were forty or fifty black ropes – at least, they looked like ropes – running along the jungle floor. The ropes ran in both directions for as far as he could see. Acting on impulse, puzzled as to what they might be, the boy decided to follow them and accordingly turned to the left.

He walked for more than a mile before the mystery was explained. The ropes weren't ropes at all. They were hair. And the boy had followed them to the scalp of their owner.

It was, of course, a giant. He was sitting outside a mud hut (from a distance, the boy had mistaken the hut for a small mountain) fast asleep. The giant was pitch black, the same colour as his remarkable hair, and this made the whiteness of his teeth seem all the more brilliant. These were the first things the boy noticed. The second was that despite the famine, the giant looked remarkably well fed.

The boy was just wondering whether he should stay where he was or head for home as fast as his feet would carry him when he became aware of a movement. The giant's eyes had opened, and he was regarding the boy with a sort of tired puzzlement.

"What are you?" he demanded, yawning.

"Please, sir . . . I'm a boy," the boy said. "I didn't mean to wake you up. I was looking for meat."

"How did you find me?"

"Well, sir . . . I followed your hair."

"You mean, you've been haring through the jungle?"

The giant roared with laughter at his own joke, the sound making the ground vibrate. The boy laughed too, although he hadn't actually thought it was very funny. But then, when somebody one hundred times as big as you makes a joke, it's probably a good idea to laugh.

"If you want meat," the giant said, when he had calmed down, "I will give it to you. But you will have to earn it. You will have to stay here and work for me."

And so the boy remained, sweeping and chopping wood for the fire. And in return for these simple tasks, the giant was true to his word and fed him with as much steak as he could eat.

There came a time, however, when the boy became homesick. It had been months since he had seen his parents and his village and so he asked the giant for permission to take a short holiday.

"Of course," the giant said. "But you must send me someone to take your place while you're gone."

"I'll do that," the boy promised and, packing his bag full of meat for the journey, he set off through the jungle.

His family was delighted to see him when he got back and were astonished to find him looking so plump and healthy. His brother in particular pressed him to say what had happened.

"If you really want to know," the boy told him, "I can help you. How would you like a job where in return for the lightest of tasks you got more meat than you knew what to do with?"

"I'd love it!" the brother said.

Then the boy told him about the giant and the hut in the jungle. The brother naturally leapt at the opportunity to take his place and set off at once.

"By the way," he asked, just before he left, "what is this giant of yours called?"

"His name is Owuo," the boy said.

Now Owuo is a West African word. And it means death.

Six weeks passed; more than enough time to cure the boy's homesickness. The trouble with home was that there still wasn't any meat and worse still, his parents expected him to join in the household chores, which meant far harder work than he had got used to with Owuo. So one day he packed his bag again and followed the path of hair back to the giant's hut.

He had expected to see his brother there, but to his surprise there was no sign of him. The giant, however, was unperturbed.

"He left a couple of days ago," he explained. "Like you, he got homesick. I'm surprised you didn't cross paths in the jungle."

"I'd have thought he'd have waited for me," the boy said.

"Forget him!" the giant cried. "I've been waiting to tell you a new joke. Have you heard the one about the Krachian, the Salagan and the Zulu . . . ?"

Time passed as pleasantly as it had before. The giant seemed perfectly content even though the boy did precious little work. And meanwhile the boy ate so much meat that he became quite fat. But once again, the only fly in the ointment was that he missed his brother and his parents. So, gathering his courage, he asked the giant if he could be allowed a second holiday.

"Very well!" the giant said. "But this time I wonder if you could send me a young girl to take your place? In fact . . . " (and here he winked) " . . . I have it in mind to take her as my wife. If you could rustle up a pretty girl, I'd like to marinate her."

"Did you say . . . marinate her, sir?" the boy asked.

"Did I?" the giant coughed and blushed. "I meant, marry her. I want to marry her!"

It was with a slight but indistinct feeling of uneasiness that the boy returned to his village. This time he was greeted with a little less pleasure. For his brother had disappeared. Despite what the giant had said, he had never returned home.

Nonetheless, the boy didn't mention the giant – for he was afraid that he would be forbidden to return to the hut if he did. It was only when he was talking to his sister one evening that he mentioned Owuo and in particular his desire for a wife.

"A wife?" the sister repeated. "If I were the wife of this Owuo, I would never have to work again. Like you, I could eat meat all day long."

"Yes, but . . . " the boy began uncertainly.

"How do I find him?" the sister interrupted.

Although the boy still felt uneasy about it, his sister

forced him to describe the path of hair, and the next morning she left, taking a servant with her.

This time the boy only waited a fortnight before he followed her back to the giant's hut. It was with a sinking feeling that he found Owuo sitting by himself, gnawing a bone.

"You're back early," the giant said.

"Yes," the boy replied. "My sister . . . ?"

"I haven't seen her or her servant for a week." The giant tossed the bone over his shoulder. "But I expect they'll turn up soon. Get yourself some supper, my boy. You must be hungry after your journey."

The boy wasn't hungry, but nodding his thanks, he went into the giant's hut where the meat was usually hung, out of the sun. As always, the ground was littered with bones and it was as he stepped over these that he stopped, a wave of ice rippling through his body. His eyes bulged. His hair stood on end. The skin at the back of his neck tried to creep onto his shoulders.

There was a bracelet made of red beads around one of the bones. He would have recognised it anywhere, for he had made it himself. He had once given it to his sister as a birthday present.

That night, as soon as it was dark, the boy tiptoed away from the hut and then, his heart pounding, raced through the jungle, crashing blindly into the undergrowth, hardly caring where he went. He didn't stop until he had somehow reached his village, and then he was so breathless that it was an hour before he could tell his parents what had happened.

The grief of the villagers at the loss of three lives was mingled with horror when they heard how Owuo had dealt with his victims. As one, they marched into the jungle, carrying with them flaming torches to light their way. The boy went with them, for although nobody had said as much, he knew that he was to blame, and there was nothing he would not do to make amends.

It was by the light of the torches that they came upon the hair, more like snakes now than ropes as it twisted through the night. Then the boy had an idea.

"Owuo is too big for us to fight," he cried. "Let the fire do our work for us."

And so saying, he seized a torch and thrust it into the hair.

Like a burning fuse, the hair hissed and crackled, carrying the fire on a winding path through the jungle. The villagers followed close behind. And so it was that they arrived at the hut just in time to see Owuo erupt in flames. One moment he was sleeping peacefully, the next he had disappeared in a crimson inferno. His screams were like the wind in a thunderstorm. But then it was all over and only a great heap of white powder showed where he had lain.

However, rummaging around in the ashes, the boy came upon a small bottle that Owuo had kept hidden in the very hair that had been his undoing. There were just four drops of a transparent liquid in the bottle and realising that whatever it was must be magic, he allowed three of them to fall on the bones in the giant's hut. In an instant, to the great rejoicing of the villagers, his brother, his sister and the servant-girl sprang to life, apparently none the worse for having been chewed up, swallowed and digested.

"Now – what shall I do with the last drop?" the boy asked.

"Wait . . ." his father said.

"No!" his mother cried.

"You idiot!" the villagers yelled.

For the boy had upturned the bottle over the ashes of the giant.

Everyone stared.

A puddle formed in the middle of the ashes, bubbling and hissing. A wisp of smoke curled poisonously upwards, writhing in the moonlight. Slowly, hideously, an eye took shape. It opened, then gazed balefully at the boy who staggered back, terrified.

But that was all. Although the potion was powerful enough to restore a human life, it could manage no more than one eye of the giant.

In Togo, where this myth originated, the people believe that the eye is still there, and that whenever it blinks, someone, somewhere in the world dies. And because there is so much dust in the country, it blinks often. And one day, they say, the eye will blink for you . . .

# INDEX OF GREEK CHARACTERS

Numbers in italics refer to the pages in the book on which the character appears.

ANTILOCHUS The youngest Greek to die at Troy *79*.

APHRODITE Goddess of love and of beauty, awarded the golden apple by Paris *30*; birth *30*; married to Hephaestus *29*; offers Helen to Paris *30*; passions of *36*; punishes Narcissus *124*; takes pity on Narcissus *126*.

APOLLO God of the sun, music, poetry, medicine and fine arts. Son of Zeus *82*; enraged by Achilles killing Troilus on his altar *80*; gives bow to Hercules *82*; and Prometheus *90*; gives lyre to Orpheus *110*.

ARACHNE Lydian girl who challenged Athene to a weaving contest and was turned into a spider for her vanity *45*.

ARGUS One-hundred-eyed monster *54*; slain by Hermes *58*.

ARIADNE Daughter of King Minos. She fell in love with Theseus and helped him kill the Minotaur *153*.

ARISTAEUS Son of Apollo and the first man to learn the art of bee keeping. Father of Actaeon *110, 160*; caused death of Eurydice *111*.

ARTEMIS Chaste goddess of the moon and the hunt *57, 164*; spots Actaeon and changes him into a stag *165*.

ASCALAPHUS Gardener in Hades *41*; betrays Persephone *42*; punished by Persephone *43*.

ATHENE Daughter of Metis and Zeus, out of whose head she sprang *28*; in judgement of Paris *26*; and Medusa *28, 101*; weaving contest against Arachne *47*; gives robe to Hercules *82*; friend of Prometheus *91*; advises Perseus on how to destroy Gorgons *103*.

ATLAS Titan condemned to support the heavens on his shoulders by Zeus *91*. Atlas was turned into stone when Perseus showed him Medusa's head − hence the Atlas mountains of North Africa.

AUGEIAS King whose stables were cleared by Hercules *82*.

BRISEIS Beautiful captive of Achilles at the siege of Troy *74*.

BUNOMUS Son of Helen and Paris *34*; death of *35*.

CALLIOPE Mother of Orpheus *110*. One of the nine

Muses, she taught pipe-playing and healing to Achilles 70.

CALLISTO Nymph slain by Artemis after being seduced by Zeus 164.

CENTAURS Half-man and half-horse, they were the sons of Centaurus, son of Apollo and Stilbia; at Peleus's wedding 22; Cheiron the Centaur 70.

CERBERUS Three-headed dog that guarded the gates of Hades; meets Orpheus 113.

CERCYON Wrestler killed by Theseus on the road to Athens 130.

CHARON Ferryman on the River Acheron in the Underworld; tricked by Orpheus 115.

CHEIRON Most famous – and most civilized – of the Centaurs 70.

CHRYSIPPUS Son of King Pelops, stolen away by King Laius of Thebes 124; death of 124.

CIRCE Enchantress whom Odysseus encountered on the island of Aeaea. Visited by Glaucus 63; turns Scylla into monster 65.

CORE Daughter of Demeter who became known as Persephone after being taken into the Underworld 37.

CYCLOPES One-eyed monsters who lived on the western side of Sicily. Employed as blacksmiths by Zeus 131; Polyphemus encounters Odysseus 133.

CYCNUS Son of Poseidon; killed by Achilles at Troy 73.

DAEDALUS Cunning architect who built the Cretan labyrinth to house the Minotaur 146; father of Icarus 146.

DANAE Mother of Perseus 99; impregnated by Zeus in a shower of coins.

DANAIDES Daughters of Danaus, tormented in the Underworld 118.

DEINO One of the three Grey Ones 104.

DEMETER Goddess of agriculture and marriage 36; mother of Persephone (Core) 37; and Erysichthon 36; and Zeus 37.

DICTYS Honest fisherman, friend of Orpheus *108*; later King of Seriphos *109*.

DIOMEDES (of Thrace) King of the Bistones and owner of four man-eating mares *83*.

DIOMEDES (of Argos) Greek soldier in the Trojan War *34*.

ECHO Nymph who wasted away for love of Narcissus *141*; punished by Hera *140*.

ENYO One of the three Grey Ones *104*.

EPIMETHEUS Unfortunate king to whom Pandora was married *95*.

ERIS Goddess of discord whose golden apple at Peleus's wedding eventually led to the Trojan War *22, 70*.

ERYSICHTHON Young man condemned to eternal hunger for cutting down a grove sacred to Demeter *36*.

EURYALE One of the three Gorgons *101*.

EURYDICE Beautiful nymph who married Orpheus *110*; dies running from Aristaeus *111*; is lost forever *121*.

EURYSTHEUS King of Mycenae for whom Hercules performed his twelve labours *82*.

GANYMEDES Most beautiful boy in the world; cup bearer to Zeus and attendant at Peleus's wedding *22*.

GLAUCUS Fisherman who turns into a merman *59*; meets Oceanus and Tethys *61*; falls in love with Scylla *62*; asks Circe for help *63*.

GORGONS Three horrible sisters – Medusa, Euryale and Sthenno – turned into monsters with snakes instead of hair by Athene *101*.

THE GREY ONES Three old crones with one eye and one tooth between them. Their names were Deino, Enyo and Pemphredo and they were sisters of the Gorgons *103*; meet Perseus *104*.

HADES God of Hades, the Underworld; brother of Zeus *37*; marries Persephone *38*; and Orpheus *118*.

HAEMON Nephew of King Laius killed by the Sphinx *122*.

**HECTOR** Eldest son of King Priam of Troy *72*; kills Patroclus *76*; killed by Achilles in single combat during the Trojan War *78*.

**HECUBA** Wife of Priam, King of Troy, and mother of Paris *25*; later enslaved by the Greeks and transformed into a dog *35*.

**HELEN** Daughter of Zeus and Leda *31*; offered to Paris by Aphrodite which sparks off the Trojan War *30*; carried off by Theseus *32*; and Ajax *32*; and Patroclus *32*; and Achilles *32*; and Prince Menelaus, her husband *32*.

**HELIOS** Sun-god who followed the sun in a golden chariot pulled by four horses *39*.

**HEPHAESTUS** Lame blacksmith god *29*; son of Hera *29*; married to Aphrodite *29*; forges shield for Hercules *82*; makes the woman Pandora for Zeus out of clay *94*.

**HERA** Goddess of marriage and the guardian of womanhood; long-suffering and often vindictive wife (and sister) of Zeus *27*; chooses Peleus for Thetis *21*; and judgement of Paris *24*; burns Semele to death *27*; has Io turned into a cow *27*, *54*; drives Hercules mad *28*; mother of Hephaestus *29*; jealous rages *36*; tries to destroy Hercules *81*; and Prometheus *91*; Ixion attempts to seduce her *118*; witnesses death of Chrysippus *125*; sends Sphinx *125*; distracted by Echo, whom she punishes *140*.

**HERCULES** Son of Zeus and Alcmene *81*; one of the most famous Greek heroes noted for his immense strength and for his twelve labours *82*; driven mad by Hera *28*; receives gifts from Poseidon, Apollo, Hermes, Athene and Hephaestus *82*.

**HERMES** Messenger-god who flew on winged sandals and carried a wand known as a caduceus; brings message to Paris *26*; sent to Underworld for Persephone *40*; and Argus *54*; father of Pan *55*; gives sword to Hercules *82*; and Prometheus *90*; carries Pandora into the world *95*.

HIPPODAMEIA Daughter of King Pelops and the supposed love of Polydectes *99*.

HIPPOLYTE Queen of the Amazons and wife of Theseus *159*.

ICARUS Son of Daedalus killed when he flew too close to the sun wearing wax wings *146*.

IDAEUS Son of Helen and Paris *34*; death of *35*.

IMMORTAL One who cannot die, usually a god *21, 68*.

IO Daughter of the river-god Inachus, who was turned into a cow by Hera *27, 54*.

IXION Cruel king, eternally bound to a wheel of fire for trying to seduce Hera *118*.

JASON Leader of the Argonauts who sailed in pursuit of the Golden Fleece *110*.

JOCASTA Widow of King Laius of Thebes who married her own son Oedipus without realising who he was *123*.

LAIUS King of Thebes *123*; uncle of Haemon *122*; killed by his son Oedipus who did not know he was his son *125*.

LEDA Zeus seduced her disguised as a swan *31*; mother of Helen *32*; wife of Tyndareus *31*.

LEOS Herald who helped Theseus to destroy the Pallantids *149*.

LYCAON Son of Priam, enslaved in the Trojan War *76*.

LYCOMEDES King of Scyros in whose court Achilles was hidden disguised as a girl *71*.

MEDUSA Most famous of the three Gorgons *101*; and Athene *28*; and her lover Poseidon *101*; killed by Perseus *108*; her head formed part of the shield of Athene.

MEMNON Ethiopian warrior killed by Achilles at Troy *79*.

MENELAUS King of Sparta and the vengeful husband of Helen *32, 71*; brother of Agamemnon.

MESTOR Son of Priam killed at Troy *76*.

METIS Wife of Zeus. He swallowed her – and this resulted in the unusual birth of Athene out of the top of his head *28*.

MIDAS King of Phrygia whose touch turned everything to gold *116*.

MINOS Son of Zeus and Europa, and King of Crete *144*;

sacrifices bull to Poseidon *145*; punished by Poseidon *145*; punishes King Aegeus *150*.

MINOTAUR Birth of *146*; monster with a human body and a bull's head kept in the Cretan labyrinth until it was killed by Theseus *158*.

MUSES Nine daughters of Zeus who inspired every creative pursuit; at Peleus's wedding *22*; Calliope teaching healing and pipe-playing to Achilles *70*; teaching Orpheus *110*. The nine Muses are: Calliope (epic poetry), Clio (history), Erato (love poetry), Euterpe (music and lyric poetry), Melpomene (tragedy), Polyhymnia (hymns and sacred music), Terpsichore (dance), Thalia (comedy), Urania (astronomy).

NARCISSUS Beautiful son of the nymph Leiriope, who fell in love with his own reflection *141*; broke Echo's heart *141*; punished by Aphrodite *141*.

NEREIDS Nymphs of the sea who come to the aid of sailors in distress *21*, *62*; Scylla *62*; Thetis *68*.

NESTOR Great warrior in the Trojan War *34*.

OCEANIDS Three thousand nymphs of the ocean who met Glaucus *62*.

OCEANUS Sea-god who welcomed Glaucus *61*.

ODYSSEUS Most famous of all the Greek heroes, condemned to wander for ten years after the war at Troy. Known for his cunning, he sometimes claimed to have invented the Trojan wooden horse *133*; at Troy *34*; frees Achilles from Scyros *71*; wounded at Troy *75*; encounters Polyphemus while returning home from Troy *133*; his story is the subject of Homer's epic poem, the *Odyssey*.

OEDIPUS Slayer of the Sphinx *125*; kills his father, King Laius *125*; marries his mother, Queen Jocasta III. Gave his name to the celebrated "Oedipus complex".

ORPHEUS Son of Calliope *110*; Apollo gives lyre *110*; lulls dragon guarding Golden Fleece *110*; marries Eurydice *110*; searches for his lost love Eurydice in the

Underworld *111*; meets Cerberus *113*; tricks Charon *115*; sees Tantalus, Tityus, Sisyphus, Ixion and the Danaides *117*; meets Hades and Persephone *118*.

PALLANTIDS Fifty sons of King Pallas *144*; kill Androgeus in Athens *147*.

PAN Half-human, half-goat son of Hermes *55*; god of shepherds, herds, fertility and growth *55*; chases Syrinx *56*.

PANDORA Woman created by Hephaestus *95*; who first let loose all the troubles in the world *97*; opens the box *97*.

PARIS Son of King Priam and Queen Hecuba *25*; while living as a shepherd he judged Aphrodite the fairest of three goddesses *26, 30, 70*; offered Helen by Aphrodite as a prize *30, 70*; kills Achilles with a poisoned arrow in the heel *80*; dies *35*.

PASIPHAE Wife of King Minos forced by Poseidon to fall in love with a bull *145*; gives birth to the Minotaur *146*.

PATROCLUS Cousin of Achilles *72*; and Helen *32*; killed by Hector at Troy *35, 76*.

PELEUS King of the Myrmidons who married Thetis *21, 68* – the only such union between a mortal and immortal in Greek mythology; father of Achilles *34, 68*.

PEMPHREDO One of the three Grey Ones *104*.

PENTHESILEIA Queen of the Amazons, killed at Troy *79*.

PERIPHETES 'Cudgel-man' killed by Theseus on the road to Athens *127*.

PERSEPHONE Daughter of Zeus *37*; kidnapped by Hades who made her Queen of the Underworld *38*; meets Orpheus *118*.

PERSEUS Son of Zeus and Danae *99*; slayer of the Gorgon Medusa *108*; accidentally killed his grandfather throwing the discus and became King of Tyrins.

POLYDECTES Cruel King of Seriphos who sent Perseus in pursuit of the Gorgon *99*; petrified *109*.

POLYPHEMUS Cyclops, or one-eyed giant, blinded by Odysseus *136*; son of Poseidon *131*.

POSEIDON Sea-god, brother of Zeus and the divine father of Theseus. The horse and the dolphin were sacred to him; gives horses to Hercules *82*; and Prometheus *90*; in love with Medusa *101*; and Minos *145*; forces Pasiphae to fall in love with a bull *145*; looks upon Theseus as his own son *151*.

PRIAM Father of Paris *24*; King of Troy during the Trojan War *73*; death of *35*.

PROCRUSTES Villain killed by Theseus on the road to Athens *130*.

PROMETHEUS Titan (race of giants) and the creator of mankind *90*; friend of Athene *91*; horribly punished for the theft of fire *93*.

PROTESILAUS First Greek to jump onto the Trojan shore and the first to die in the Trojan War *72*.

SCIRON Another of the rogues killed by Theseus on the road to Athens *128*.

SCYLLA Nereid, beloved of Glaucus *62*; turned into a monster by Circe *66*.

SEMELE Mortal loved by Zeus but burnt to death through the trickery of Hera *27*.

SINIS "Pine-bender" killed by Theseus on the road to Athens *127*; son of Procrustes *128*.

SISYPHUS Prisoner in the Underworld, punished for betraying Zeus *117*.

SPHINX Monster with the head and breasts of a woman, the body of a lion, the tail of a serpent, the wings of a bird, and a human voice. Sent by Hera to guard the road to Thebes: famous for its riddle *122*. There is a colossal statue of the Sphinx at Giza.

STHENNO One of the three Gorgons *101*.

SYRINX Nymph loved by Pan *56*.

TANTALUS Another doomed soul in the Underworld – in his case for serving the gods a cannibalistic feast *117*.

TETHYS Minor sea-god who welcomed Glaucus *61*.

THESEUS Son of King Aegeus and Aethra *130, 148*; carries off Helen *32*; kills Procrustes, Periphetes, Sinis, Cercyon, Sciron *130*; sets sail for Knossos *151*; helped by Ariadne *153*; slays the Minotaur *158*.

THETIS Nereid, the mother of Achilles *34, 68*; for a short time the wife of Peleus *21, 68*.

TIRESIAS Prophet struck blind by Athene *29. 47*; foretells Narcissus's fate *139*.

TITYUS Giant pegged out in the Underworld for trying to violate the Titaness Leto *117*.

TROILUS Son of Priam, slain by Achilles during the Trojan War *76, 80*.

TYNDAREUS King of Sparta and husband of Leda *31*.

ZEUS King of the gods and goddesses on Mount Olympus, son of Leto *117*; husband of Hera *27*; lover of Metis (his first wife) *28*, Leda *31*, Demeter *37*, Alcmene *81*, Callisto *164*; father of Athene by Metis *28*, Helen by Leda *32*, Persephone by Demeter *37*, Hercules by Alcmene *81*, Minos *144*, Aphrodite *30*, Apollo *82*, and Artemis, the Muses *22* and the Fates; brother of Hades *37*; and Prometheus *90*; betrayed by Sisyphus *117*; employed Cyclopes as blacksmiths *131*; slips away while Echo distracts Hera *140*.

# INDEX OF NON-GREEK CHARACTERS

Numbers in italics refer to the pages in the book on which the character appears.

ARTHUR (Celtic) Legendary king of Britain who presided over the Knights of the Round Table at Camelot *188*; sets out on a quest with Gawain *191*.

ASHWAPATI (Indian) Father of Princess Savitri *223*

BEOWULF (Anglo-Saxon) Slayer of the Grendel *183*. He is the subject of an epic poem dating from the eighth century.

BODVILD (Scandinavian) Daughter of King Nidud; loved Volund the Blacksmith *201*; is destroyed *202*.

EDGETHEOW (Anglo-Saxon) Father of Beowulf *184*.

FAUSTULUS (Roman) Shepherd who found Romulus and Remus and became their foster father *170*.

FREYA (Scandinavian) Goddess of love and marriage who lived in Asgard *209*; Friday is named after her.

GAWAIN (Celtic) Nephew of King Arthur and a knight of the Round Table *188*; sets out on a quest with King Arthur *191*.

SAINT GEORGE (English) Patron saint of England who defeated the dragon at Silene *175*.

GERIGUIAGUIATUGO (Bororo Indian) Worthless wretch. The 'hero' of many stories told by the Bororo Indians of South America *253*.

GRENDEL (Anglo-Saxon) In the poem *Beowulf*, the monster descended from Cain that terrorised Denmark *182*; killed by Beowulf *186*.

GROMER SOMER JOURE (Celtic) Servant of Morgan le Fay who introduced fear to King Arthur *189*; brother of the ugly wife *197*.

HERVOR (Scandinavian) Valkyrie or warrior maiden married to Volund the blacksmith *199*.

HORUS (Egyptian) Latin form of the name of the sun-god Hor. He avenged the murder of his father Osiris *8*.

HROTHGAR (Anglo-Saxon) King of Denmark and the creator of Heorot Hall *181*; meets Beowulf *183*.

HYGELAC (Anglo-Saxon) King of the Geats at the time of

Beowulf *184.*

INTI (Inca) God of the Sun and father of Manco Capac *266.*

ISIS (Egyptian) Sister-wife of Osiris and the goddess of womanhood *7.* She is said to have invented mummification.

IZANAGI (Japanese) Father of the gods. He and Izanami were the first divine couple in Japanese mythology *241.*

IZANAMI (Japanese) Wife of Izanagi. She died giving birth to the god of fire *241.*

JADE (Chinese) Emperor and Lord of the Sky who first created man from clay, also called Tung Wang Kung *238.*

JOSEPHUS (Roman) Bandit leader who inadvertently brought Remus to his grandfather Numitor *170.*

KO-AI (Chinese) Kuan Yu's daughter *232;* death of *234.*

KUAN YU (Chinese) Bell-maker who cast the great bell of Peking *230.*

KUO PO (Chinese) Celebrated magician who predicts the fate of Kuan Yu's bell *233.*

LAOZI (Chinese) Another magician; the tutor of Sun Hou-Tzu *238.*

LOKI (Norse) Mischievous god of firelight. A blood-brother of Odin and occasional ally of Thor *209.*

MANCO CAPAC (Inca) Son of Inti who founded the Inca empire *267.*

MARS (Roman) God of battle and father of Romulus and Remus *169.* The month of March is named after him.

MAUI (Polynesian) Trickster-hero, responsible for the discovery of New Zealand *271.*

MAUI-POE (Polynesian) Brother of Maui *272.*

MAUI-ROTO (Polynesian) Brother of Maui *272.*

MAUI-TAHA (Polynesian) Brother of Maui *272.*

MAUI-WAHO (Polynesian) Brother of Maui *272.*

MJOLNIR (Norse) Magic hammer of Thor *214.*

MONKEY (Chinese) See SUN HOU-TZU.

MORGAN LE FAY (Celtic) The evil queen who bewitched Arthur *189;* destroyed *194.*

MURI-RANGA-WHENUA (Polynesian) Gave Maui a magic jawbone with which he fished New Zealand out of the sea *272*.

NARADA (Indian) Holy man in the court of King Ashwapati who predicts the death of Savitri's husband *225*.

NIDUD (Norse) Cruel king who kept Volund imprisoned *198*; is driven mad *206*.

NORNAGEST (Norse) Name means 'protected by the Norns'. A poet and singer and perhaps one of the last of the heroes *207*; death of *213*.

NORNS (Norse) Three female spirits who were mistresses of fate. They were: Urd (the past), Verdandi (the present), and the dreaded Skuld (the future) who cast an evil spell on Nornagest *207*.

NUMITOR (Roman) King of Alba Longa whose throne was seized by his brother Amulius. Grandfather of Romulus and Remus *169*.

OCCLO HUACO (Inca) Sister and wife of Manco Capac *267*.

ODIN (Norse) God of war; who ruled over the gods in the great citadel of Asgard. The father of Thor *209, 214*.

OLAF TRYGGVASON (Norse) King of Norway (AD 997–1000) *210*; Nornagest sings in his court *210*; kills Nornagest *213*.

OSIRIS (Egyptian) God of fertility who was cut into pieces by his brother Set, but restored by Isis *7*.

OWUO (West African) Giant; the personification of death *279*.

PYRAMUS (Babylonian) Youth who died for love of Thisbe *14*.

RA (Egyptian) The sun-god and father of the first divine couple. All living creatures were created from his tears *7*.

REMUS (Roman) Son of Mars and Rhea Silvia *169*; twin brother of Romulus, killed by Romulus during the building of Rome *173*.

RHEA SILVIA (Roman) Daughter of Numitor, forced into becoming a Vestal Virgin by Amulius *169*; mother of Romulus and Remus *169*.

ROMULUS (Roman) Twin brother of Remus who founded the city of Rome *172*; the son of Mars and Rhea Silvia *169*; killed Remus *173*.

SATYAVAN (Indian) Husband of Savitri *224*.

SAVITRI (Indian) Princess whose devotion to her husband saved him from death. The Indian equivalent of the Greek heroine Alcestis *223*.

SEDNA (Eskimo) Sea goddess whose severed fingers made whales and seals. She was briefly married to a bird *260*.

SEMIRAMIS (Babylonian) King at the time of Pyramus and Thisbe *14*.

SET (Egyptian) Evil brother of Osiris who ruled Egypt until he was killed by Horus *9*.

SKULD (Scandinavian) The most feared of the three female spirits called Norns. Skuld was the spirit of the future *207*.

SUN HOU-TZU (Chinese) Hero of the Hsi yu chi and a popular character in much Chinese literature. Tried to defy the Buddha *237*. Otherwise known as Monkey.

SUSANOO (Japanese) God of the sea, thunder and fertility *241*; headstrong brother of Amaterasu, cast out of Heaven because of his destructive nature *243*.

TAMA-HUI-KI-TE-RANGI (Polynesian) God, ancestor of Maui *271*.

THISBE (Babylonian) Lover of Pyramus who died at the tomb of Ninus *14*.

THOR (Norse) Son of Odin. The god of the sky and of thunder and the possessor of the magic hammer Mjolnir *209*.

THRYM (Norse) King of the giants in Jotunheim *215*; slain by Thor for stealing his magic hammer *222*.

URD (Norse) One of the three female spirits called Norns.

Urd was the spirit of the past *207*.

VERDANDI (Norse) One of the three female spirits called Norns. Verdandi was the spirit of the present *207*.

VOLUND (Norse) Blacksmith *198*; is captured by Nidud *199*; plots his revenge *200*.

WEALTHEOW (Anglo-Saxon) Hrothgar's Queen of Denmark *181*.

YAMA (Indian) God of death *225*; is tricked by Savitri *228*.

YUNG LO (Chinese) Emperor of China at the time of the casting of the bell of Peking *230*.